KU-310-527

the plan buy cook book

4+2+1 = dinner done

Plan once, eat well all week

Jen Petrovic and Gaby Chapman

Hardie Grant

BOOKS

OИО

For our families:
Eddie, Lachlan and Lucy
Simon, Luca, Alex and Evan
and all the PlanBuyCook app users

Who Is This Book For?

Do you panic about what's for dinner every night at 5 pm?

Do you shop for food three or more times a week?

Are you tired of serving the same meals over and over again to your family?

Have you got a fridge full of food, but nothing to cook?

Are you sick of buying food that you throw out?

Are you procrastibaking* instead of getting on with the main meal?

Let's face it: you have hit the wall, just like Gaby had before she met Jen and they started their meal-planning app PlanBuyCook.

You want to provide nutritious food for your family but are finding the daily dinner a grind. You might even have a fussy eater to satisfy.

You work either part-time or full-time, or you are a stay-at-home parent struggling with cooking the family meals.

You want to cut down your food waste and cut out multiple trips to the supermarket each week. Saving money on your shopping is a bonus.

You need a plan to manage the week that eases your mental load.

This book is for families everywhere who are struggling with the process of getting a healthy, tasty meal on the table every night at a reasonable hour.

Our Dinner Done = 4+2+1 formula will cut your cooking time in half. It will most likely change your life, like it has for Gaby and for so many others. We hope it will lead to a lifetime of fuss-free planning, buying, cooking and eating habits for you and your family.

Plan once, eat well all week. Dinner Done.

*Procrastibaking: verb, the art of putting off cooking the evening meal and baking instead.

Contents

About the Authors

Meet Jen and Gaby, the team behind PlanBuyCook and the Dinner Done = 4+2+1 formula.

Gaby is a mother of three boys, and she always panicked about what was for dinner. She was running her own business and juggling her kids' activities with work and family life – and struggling with all of them. Her cookbook collection was of no help: too many ingredients or too complicated methods for weeknight cooking. She would ring her friends at 5 pm some nights in a fluster trying to gather other people's ideas, then frantically run to the supermarket to buy the ingredients, inevitably forgetting something. Add a fussy eater to the mix, and it was a recipe for disaster. Dinner was served up late each night to tired and cranky kids. That was, until she met Jen.

Jen is a chef, master meal planner, mother of two and the most organised person ever. She has worked as a restaurant chef, in large-scale catering and as a personal chef. In short, she knows how to get a meal on the table without too much stress. Once she had children, she needed to adjust her cooking for the everyday: food that tasted great but was also good for growing kids. Restaurant food with loads of components is fine for special occasions, but hopeless for weeknights. So she worked on ways to simplify recipes, while also teaching the mums in her mums' group how to greatly reduce food waste, store food well and save time in the kitchen.

A chance conversation with a group of school mums about the hassle of the evening meal led Jen and Gaby to build an app to help solve the nightly 'What's for dinner?' dilemma. Together, they built PlanBuyCook, one of Apple's top-selling meal-planning apps. They have now brought together their know-how in this book to give families a simple formula to get dinner done every night without fuss and without breaking the bank.

Introduction

Feeding a family is quite a shock. It turns out they need to eat three times a day (or more), for the best part of 20+ years. Who knew?

Not everyone is born into a family that knows how to cook well (neither of us were). And, importantly, very few families have any idea how to really plan meals and cook with ease, how to produce tasty, healthy meals every day from the food in their house without fuss and in a timely way. That's where this book comes in.

Home cooking doesn't need to be stressful or difficult. This is a book about how to simplify your life and cut down the time spent on weekday cooking, using a proven formula for success. It will take you from when your kids are young through to teaching them to plan, shop to a budget and cook for themselves by the time they leave home.

This is not your typical cookbook with fancy breakfasts and delicious desserts. For a start, it just has dinner recipes. But it also has information on banishing the 5 pm panic and the daily dinner grind forever. It will cut your shopping and weekday cooking time in half and improve your cooking skills. Most importantly, our 4+2+1 formula makes getting dinner done simple.

We show you how to get dinner done in the following sections:

THE BASICS: The 4+2+1 formula.

PLAN: Getting started, seasonal sample meal plans and how to plan your cooking week.

BUY: How to shop and save, pantry and refrigerator staples and kitchen tools.

COOK: We bring it all together with 80+ recipes for meals everyone will enjoy, in different categories: Double-Up Meals, Fast & Fresh Meals, BBQ Salad recipes, Speedy Sides and Super Simple Meals.

Gaby takes you through the Basics, Plan and Buy sections, and Jen through the Cook section.

You might choose to read the book section by section, or drop in and out of various parts at the front. You might even take the basics of the Plan section and apply the 4+2+1 formula to your own recipes.

You might be like Gaby and have a million cookbooks but nothing to cook for dinner. Or you could be like Jen, who can glance at a food photo and know how to cook it. But getting dinner done is neither about your cooking ability nor the number of cookbooks you own. It is about being a little bit organised, having some meal-planning know-how, using recipes everyone enjoys, having the ingredients at home to cook them, and getting savvy about cooking to match your lifestyle.

Don't worry if your kids are now teenagers, or you don't have any children. It is never too late to learn good food habits, how to cook from scratch, time-savers in the kitchen and life skills like food budgeting. Our foolproof formula works for households of one through to larger or multi-generational families.

You can take it further by downloading the PlanBuyCook app, which will allow you to plan your meals, double freezable meals, generate your shopping list like magic and scale each dinner to match your household size, from 1 to 10 serves.

Reading this book is your first step towards freedom from dinner being a burden and into a world where the evening meal is just a habit and a small part of what you do – quickly and simply – every day, no matter how much chaos is going on around you.

What's All the Fuss About Home Cooking?

Some people may be wondering why home cooking is so important. Here are a few great reasons why you should cook more at home, and how the 4+2+1 formula can help you get organised.

IT SAVES TIME

Going to the shops daily or three times a week takes up so much time. Making a plan that fits into your life and shopping just once a week allows you to reclaim your time.

IT SAVES STRESS

There is no doubt about it: not knowing what you are having for dinner can play on your mind all day. And cooking with tired and hungry kids around only adds to the craziness. So, ease the load with a simple meal plan for fast weekday cooking.

HELPS BEAT OBESITY

Food writer Michael Pollan nailed it when he said that the only countries where morbid obesity is an issue are those where home cooking is no longer the norm. Also, the more you cook, the less you eat. Sounds odd, right? But if you increase your home cooking, you will reduce the amount you eat as you control the portions.

YOU KNOW WHAT YOU ARE EATING

When you cook food yourself, you have complete control over the ingredients that you and your family consume, whether that be the quantity of salt, fat and sugar, or any number of preservatives, flavour enhancers and artificial sweeteners.

IT MAKES DOLLARS AND SENSE

Not only will home cooking save your waistline, it will also save you money. Our easy-to-follow plan can save households, on average, around $2500 a year or more.

IT'S GOOD FOR THE ENVIRONMENT

We all need to stop throwing out food. Most of our food waste was edible at the time we threw it in the bin, and it is now producing tonnes of CO_2 in the process of decomposing in landfill. You will cut down your edible food waste and food packaging by using our formula.

That's why we developed the 4+2+1 plan: to make it easier for you to bring more home cooking into your life. So, let's show you how to get dinner done easily, by covering the basics of 4+2+1.

"People who can plan, improvise, maintain the inventory on their freezer, fridge and pantry, and minimise waste by using leftover food tend to have better dietary patterns. They are also more likely to spend less on takeaway foods. Being a boss of your own kitchen is a life skill everyone should learn."

– Professor Clare Collins, Dietitian, University of Newcastle

The Basics of 4+2+1 Cooking

Dinner Done = 4+2+1 Explained

4+2+1 is not a diet, nor is it designed to make you quit anything except worrying about the evening meal. It is simply a way to incorporate better planning, buying and cooking-from-scratch habits for a fuss-free life. It can be adapted to any diet or recipes with ease.

THIS IS OUR MEAL-PLANNING 4+2+1 FORMULA

 x4

Cook 4 meals from scratch each week: 2 Double-Up meals and 2 Fast & Fresh

Double-Up two meals each week. Eat two this week and freeze the rest. The remaining two meals should be Fast & Fresh. These are meals that you can make in under an hour.

 x2

Take 2 Foodbanked meals from the freezer

Simply toss together a salad, or cook some pasta, rice, or vegetables to accompany your defrosted Foodbanked meal on the night as required.

 x1

Have 1 Super Simple meal

Leftovers, takeaway or something easy like toasted sandwiches or eggs on toast will round out your week.

Having a formula doesn't mean you are tied to set meals on set nights; you can vary your plan as long as you have the ingredients. You can also either choose to use some of our fabulous and varied meals, or substitute some with your own recipes. It will work either way.

THE SECRET

The key is to 'Double-Up' two recipes – cook twice as much as you need – to make two freezable meals each week. Plan to eat one of each of these meals this week and freeze the other meals for eating two weeks down the track. We call this 'Foodbanking'.

Double-Up meals might be substantial one-pot meals like our Chicken & Chorizo Braise (page 71), or pasta sauces that go into the freezer as nearly complete meals, or basics like Hamburgers (page 88), Lamb Kibbeh (page 97) or any of our marinated meat recipes that can be frozen uncooked. Or they might be pantry meals or soups. You need to put two meals in the freezer each week to achieve freedom from the daily dinner grind.

The other two meals you make from scratch during the week should be 'Fast & Fresh': meals that don't take a lot of preparation and cooking time. The key to these meals is having the ingredients on hand, ready to go.

Importantly, you also need to plan to eat two Foodbanked meals each week to save you cooking time. You should use your previously Foodbanked meals within two weeks to keep everything on high rotation. This way, you are not stockpiling food that takes up freezer space, and you are still keeping variety in your cooking by having meals from two weeks before.

And because we are all about simplicity, we also include what we call a 'Super Simple' meal in the mix. This might be leftovers, takeaway or something like eggs on toast, toasted sandwiches, jacket potatoes or flatbread pizzas. Plan to make one Super Simple meal each week that anyone in the family can cook.

7 NIGHTS OF DINNER DONE = 4+2+1.

With this, you should be able to do all your cooking in about two hours when time is really tight during the working week, instead of the countless hours you now spend thinking about, shopping for and cooking meals each week.

You can use your own recipes, or try ours (pages 65–215). To know if your regular recipes can be doubled up and frozen, go to page 25 for our quick guide.

Our Cook section is divided into Double-Up meals (page 68), Fast & Fresh meals (page 144) and Super Simple meals (page 208). We have also included handy Speedy Sides (page 204) and BBQ Salads (page 194) to accompany any of your meals.

The recipes include a range of cuisines, from European, Middle Eastern and Asian to Mexican, as well as family favourites such as hamburgers. They are designed to expand your cooking repertoire through simple techniques using ingredients readily found in the supermarket.

The Meals

DOUBLE-UP MEALS

Doubling up and freezing meals for later is the best and simplest way to cut down cooking time. It sounds obvious, but Foodbanking meals each week was something I had never put into practice until starting PlanBuyCook.

I can't describe the joy of pulling a ready-made home-cooked meal from the freezer on a busy weeknight and only having to reheat and make some sides to accompany it. That's dinner done in 15 minutes or less.

It can sometimes be tempting to freeze a lot of meals, but only do so if you have plenty of freezer space. Doubling up two freezable meals each week will give you a great range of food and still keep your menu fresh. If you can get up to four frozen home-cooked meals in your Foodbank, you should never be short on a great variety of faster-than-takeaway, nourishing home-cooked dinners.

Marinades

The Double-Up section includes marinades that are also great to Foodbank. Once you get home from the shops, marinate your meat straight away or the next day (doubling up the quantities of course), freeze one meal and keep the other meal in the fridge to eat that week. Your Foodbanked meat will marinate while freezing, and again while defrosting, saving you those annoying 4+ hours that it takes to marinate meat properly. This is one of our most popular tips, and helps make your Foodbanked meal quick and easy to prepare.

Pantry Meals

Pantry meals (almost exclusively) use ingredients from the pantry. These meals are perfect to put on the plan at least once a month. As we all know, plans regularly change, and we often end up with too much food and not enough nights to cook it, or extra people drop by unexpectedly and you have nothing to cook. If you have ingredients for a few pantry meals on hand, you won't struggle to produce an extra meal out of nowhere if you need to.

DOUBLE YOUR MEALS EASILY
The PlanBuyCook app allows you to double up the quantities of your freezable meals and automatically adds them to your shopping list.

GET ON THE FAST & FRESH EXPRESS

Developing a good repertoire of Fast & Fresh meals – dinners that can be prepped and cooked in less than one hour from start to finish – will really save you time in the kitchen. Some take only a fraction of that time, while others will take close to the hour. But all are guaranteed to be easy, super tasty and, once you are done cooking, you won't need an eternity to clean up. The more you make the recipes, the faster it will be to cook them.

Choose your two Fast & Fresh meals based on their cooking time to match your available time that day.

You will probably notice that our Fast & Fresh section includes a number of Asian-style recipes, which some people may have traditionally avoided due to not being confident with the ingredients and techniques. Buy a wok, keep some core sauces in the pantry and fridge (see pages 58–9), and you'll be able to make a quick stir-fry or noodle dish without any fuss.

SUPER SIMPLE MEAL IDEAS

Make one meal a week Super Simple: something as easy as toasted sandwiches, eggs on toast, sausages and mash, leftovers or takeaway. And guess what? You don't need to be the cook on Super Simple meal night; almost anyone in the house can prepare them.

If you like routine, make your Super Simple meal night the same each week – on your busiest night. Or mix it up each week depending on your schedule.

TRICKS OF 4+2+1 MEAL PLANNING

Mastering the basics of meal planning the 4+2+1 way involves embracing some changes to making your everyday meals.

———————————————

- Cook two meals at once
- Be kitchen confident
- Shop well, shop once
- Make the freezer your (best) friend
- Love your leftovers
- Get storage savvy
- Lighten the load

———————————————

Read on for more on each of these …

Cook Two Meals at Once

There is only one sure-fire way to make your weekday cooking easy, and that is making some meals in advance on the weekend or your day off. As it is quite likely that you will have more time on the weekend than the weekdays, this is the ideal opportunity to make at least one Double-Up meal, plus one other meal for the week.

Since a number of Double-Up meals are braises and take longer to cook, it is good to use the time while they are in the oven or on the stove to make a second meal for the week. Whether the extra meal is a Fast & Fresh meal or another Double-Up meal, you will be maximising your time-saving by making three or four meals in the time it would usually take to cook one.

Jen often cooks in bulk on a Sunday afternoon and may not eat one of the cooked meals until Wednesday. She stores the food in the fridge until then. If plans change, she'll simply shift that meal to the freezer for eating later.

I quite like to cook two Double-Up meals on a Sunday, particularly in winter, to get the bulk of the cooking over and done with. Winter is great for slow-cooked meals, and it is quite nice being in the warmth of the kitchen.

In summer, one of my Double-Up meals is often marinated meat, which only takes about 5 minutes to prepare. So, when it is hot outside, making two Double-Up meals doesn't require as much time as it does in the cooler months when you are more interested in eating slow-cooked food.

Save time when cooking multiple meals by chopping all the prep ingredients, such as onions and carrots, at the same time. Keep them in separate piles or dishes to ensure you have the right amount for each meal.

Learning to chop onions like a chef will save you so much time in the kitchen.

Be Kitchen Confident

The weird thing about home cooking becoming a mainstream television event – think *Masterchef* and other kitchen reality shows – is that many people lose confidence in their everyday cooking skills when they watch these shows. Can't temper chocolate by the age of 10? What have you been doing with your life? In many ways, they have made us doubt our abilities in the kitchen, which makes us even less likely to cook at home or try new things.

I used to only cook a meal if I had every ingredient on hand. Just one missing item and I'd desperately try to rustle up the ingredients for a different meal at short notice, or rush to the shops instead. This was an expensive and time-wasting way to get a meal on the table.

Getting dinner done regularly and using some of Jen's cooking hacks will help build your confidence in the kitchen. The more you cook, the more comfortable you'll become, and the less you'll worry about having the exact ingredients. Jen has written some tips, shortcuts and suggestions for replacement ingredients throughout the Cook section to help build your cooking know-how and skills.

And, if in doubt, leave it out. Not many everyday dinner recipes will fail without a small ingredient. Get dinner done without it, rather than trying to find another meal at short notice.

Mastering some really basic skills like chopping an onion and feeling confident in replacing a missing ingredient (or going without it) will make cooking far less stressful.

Speedy Sides

Did anyone ever teach you how to steam rice to perfection every time? Need a go-to salad dressing that will suit any leafy greens? You have come to the right place.

I come from a family of pretty average cooks (sorry Mum and Dad) – generations of them, in fact (yep, my grandparents too). In all honesty, it wasn't until I worked with Jen that I really gained complete confidence in steaming rice without a rice cooker, or whipping up a great salad on short notice without consulting a cookbook each time.

Many handy cooking basics, including how to steam rice, cook couscous, steam and boil veg, steam Asian greens and make quick salad dressings can be found in the Speedy Sides section (page 204).

Shop Well, Shop Once

Many people go food shopping three times a week or more. In fact, we often spend more time shopping than cooking. Not having the fresh ingredients you need in your kitchen limits the types of meals you can make, and often tempts you to reach for processed, ready-made food that is high in sugar and fat.

We are all guilty of heading to the shops without a definitive plan, only to find ourselves picking up random ingredients to cobble together some meals for the next few days. Meal planning can put a stop to this and save you time and money. Here are our tips:

- Have a list and stick to it. Only buy what's on the list, unless you find a great special on a food that you can freeze, such as meat, or a pantry item you have the storage space for.
- Reduce supermarket visits to once a week. A little bit of organisation with one larger shop will save you time and money. If you run out of fruit and vegetables later in the week, then buy extra at a green grocer where you won't be tempted to make impulse purchases.
- Try online shopping, as you only buy what you need rather than being tempted by additional (usually non-planned) items at the end of the aisles or at the checkout.
- Discount supermarkets and generic brands can save you quite a bit of money. Try them to see whether they suit your taste.

- Plant fresh herbs in your garden. Herbs add great flavour to your cooking, but they are expensive to buy. The added bonus in growing your own is that you only pick what you need for each meal.
- Don't buy fresh ingredients without thinking about how they will be used, unless they freeze well. They will often end up in the compost or bin. That eggplant that looks amazing in the supermarket will look less great at the end of the week if you haven't planned a meal to use it in.
- Keep your pantry stocked with staples such as tinned tomatoes, garlic, onions and pasta for an emergency meal.
- If you have the storage space, buying pantry goods in bulk can save money. But beware of buying too much, or buying items you're unlikely to use, as they too will end up in the rubbish when you haven't touched them two years down the track.

 Don't shop when you are hungry; you'll buy more than you need.

Make the Freezer Your (Best) Friend

One of our secrets to stress-free cooking is using the freezer well. I remember the first time Jen showed me her freezer of home-cooked meals waiting to defrost when she needed them, and interesting ingredients like pine nuts and curry leaves. My freezer, on the other hand, was filled with unlabelled raw meat (did I buy lamb or beef, and why didn't I write it on the bag?), some ice blocks and a few bags of frozen vegetables.

Using your freezer well means having a few Foodbanked Double-Up meals on hand (ideally up to four), some marinated meats ready to defrost and cook, popular ingredients (such as frozen fresh breadcrumbs, bacon and fresh chillies), and even some loaves of bread if you have room. This will save an extra visit to the supermarket each week.

The other must-have item in your freezer if you have kinder- or school-aged children is lunchbox snacks. We recommend making a snack each weekend (outsource this task to willing children who generally enjoy baking sweet and savoury treats) and freezing it, already cut into portions, ready for the week's lunchboxes. Get the treats into the freezer quickly to stop hungry little people grazing on them. They will defrost in the lunchbox in time for 'little lunch', aka morning tea.

Upgrading your fridge? Look for one with a good-sized freezer to make it meal-planning friendly. Or you might even have room for a deep-freeze if you like to store meat in bulk.

Plan Buy Cook

WHAT MAKES A MEAL FREEZABLE?

You can find all our Double-Up meals on pages 68–143, but what about your own recipes? How can you tell which ones will freeze well?

Most slow-cooked braised meals are perfect for freezing. If making pies – whether topped with mash or pastry – simply double up the filling and freeze, ready for assembling and topping later.

As a general rule, meals with beans and lentils also freeze well. Pasta sauces, particularly those using tomato as a base, are also great for Foodbanking.

Raw or cooked marinated meats freeze really well. Move your frozen marinated meat to the fridge the night before you want to cook it and it should be defrosted by the next evening.

As a general guide, we tend to avoid freezing rice and potato, but that is largely personal preference. So, where meals require rice or potato in the main part of the dish, we suggest freezing the dish without them, then completing the missing elements once the meal has defrosted.

Meals that don't freeze well include ingredients with a high water content, such as tofu or fish. They don't take very long to cook anyway, so keep your tofu and fish meals for Fast & Fresh nights. Stir-fries don't freeze well either – again, they are quick to cook, so you won't be cutting down on any cooking time by freezing these meals.

EVER THOUGHT OF FREEZING ... ?

- Egg whites in freezer bags
- Lemon and lime juice in ice cube trays when the fruit is cheap and in season
- Milk
- Bread
- Breadcrumbs
- Caramelised onions (see page 211)
- Diced, cooked onions for any recipe base
- Chillies (they are easier to slice when they are frozen)
- Lemongrass
- Pine nuts
- Ripe bananas and berries for smoothies, banana bread and cakes
- Kaffir lime leaves
- Curry leaves
- Wilted spinach
- Blanched vegetables
- Bacon
- Poached chicken, shredded, ready for sandwiches or salads
- Cookie dough in a roll
- Leftover stock

Love Your Leftovers

Leftovers used to lurk in my fridge for days until I got scared of them and eventually threw them out on bin night. Food accounts for half of the general waste thrown out each week in Australia, and at least 20 per cent of the edible food we buy *each week* is being thrown out. Conservative estimates put the figure at $2500 worth of food per year. So not only is it bad for the environment, it costs us money.

POT-LUCK LEFTOVERS MEAL

Some weeks, Jen has a leftovers night where her Super Simple meal is made out of pot-luck leftovers: everyone has something different from what's left of that week's meals (there are often leftovers from several meals). She simply cooks some extra vegetables to bulk out the leftovers if the meal is a bit light on. Bingo – another meal that doesn't require cooking.

If you are at all worried about the fridge shelf life of any leftover meals, simply freeze them until you are ready to eat them. Generally, home-cooked food is fine to eat for up to four days after cooking it when stored in the fridge.

Don't have enough for a family meal of pot-luck leftovers? With my family of five, we don't always have enough to make a pot-luck meal for all of us. So, I use leftovers as pre-training early dinners when one of the kids has sport around dinnertime. Then I am not under pressure to have a meal on the table at 5.30 pm when I am getting home from work. Or I take leftovers to work for lunch and watch the savings add up.

RESCUING LEFTOVER INGREDIENTS

Got random ingredients left over? Here's how to store or use them to avoid food waste.

Bread

Freeze old bread for making into breadcrumbs. Blitz in a food processor or hand-grate and store in the freezer until ready to use.

Bananas and Berries

Frozen old bananas (peeled) and ageing berries are great for smoothies, banana bread or muffins.

Takeaway Leftovers

You never know how long your takeaway food has been stored at the restaurant before you bought it, so it's best to reheat it well and use for lunch or dinner the next day.

Tomatoes

Soft tomatoes can be cut into cubes and added to your Tasty Bolognese Sauce (see page 83), Chilli con Carne (page 87), Puttanesca Sauce (page 140) or Napolitana Pasta Sauce (page 114).

Spinach

Wilt any spinach you won't eat in time and freeze until ready to use. Great for Spanakopita (page 174) or Lamb Curry (page 105).

Celery

Cut celery into batons for snacks, smoothies and juices, or dice and freeze it for use in recipes.

Vegetables

Bake or chargrill leftover vegetables such as zucchini, capsicum, pumpkin, mushrooms and eggplant to go in salads, use as pizza toppings or in a Vegetable Lasagne (page 109).

Chicken

Poach chicken before it goes to waste. Shred and store it in the freezer for sandwiches, or to add to a salad.

Bacon

Buy bacon in bulk and store it in portions in the freezer. Only defrost the portions you need.

Onions

Regularly have half an onion smelling up your fridge? Think about buying shallots as an alternative to onions when you only need smaller amounts, or dice, cook and freeze leftover onions.

Tomato Paste

Buy tomato paste in a jar, use what you need, then add a layer of olive oil (about 1 cm/½ in) to the top of the paste after each use to stop it from growing mould. Genius.

Cheese Rind

Store leftover parmesan rind in the fridge until ready to use in soups such as Minestrone (page 117) or any pasta sauce for extra flavour.

Fresh Herbs

Where possible, plan to use fresh herbs in two meals in the same week to avoid waste.

STORING HERBS AND LOOSE-LEAF LETTUCE

Pick and wash fresh leafy herbs, then store them in a sealed container between sheets of dry paper towel. Same applies to loose-leaf lettuce. Spin it in a salad spinner if you have one to dry it out once washed. You can also use the salad spinner as a storage container.

Get Storage Savvy

Wondering how to get your food to the right temperature to freeze it? Not sure about the best way to defrost? Here's the low-down on safe food handling.

STORING HOME-COOKED FOOD

It is generally safe to store home-cooked food for up to four days in the fridge. Change of plans? Move it to the freezer.

Meat you have marinated (raw) can usually stay in the fridge for two to three days.

CHILLING FOODS

When doubling up recipes and cooking in bulk, it's important to cool the food to fridge temperature, which is 4°C (39°F), before putting it in the freezer.

If you put a large volume of steaming hot food in the fridge or freezer, it cools on top and the sides, but heat can be trapped in the middle, putting food in the danger zone where bacteria can grow.

The easiest way to cool Doubled-Up food rapidly is to divide the food into two meals. If you are serving some immediately, you can keep one meal in the pot. Put the other meal into a shallow container with a large surface area. Leave it uncovered on the bench until it stops steaming when stirred (about 30 minutes to 1 hour). A cake rack underneath the container also helps to cool it quicker. Cover, place in the fridge, then move the container to the freezer the next day.

If you have cooked a Double-Up meal in the late evening and you are ready for bed, split the dish into two or three shallow containers and leave them on the bench for around 30 minutes on top of a rack, then place them in the fridge and leave uncovered – don't worry if they're still steaming slightly. Cover in the morning so the food doesn't dry out, then move to the freezer.

Food should be kept above 60°C (140°F) or below 5°C (41°F), according to current Australian government guidelines.

The danger zone in the middle is what you need to avoid.

HOW TO DEFROST FOOD SAFELY

The safest way to defrost food is in your fridge. The key is remembering to move it from the freezer to the fridge the day before you plan to eat it.

Forgotten to move your food into the fridge or plans have changed? The other way is to defrost it using your microwave.

Avoid leaving food out on the bench to defrost – it is generally not considered safe.

Match your storage container size as closely as possible to the amount of food you are freezing to avoid 'freezer burn' (discolouration due to air reaching the food).

CONTAINER OPTIONS

Looking for the best containers to store your extra meals in? Getting started with 4+2+1 meal planning does require working out the best storage options for your freezer. The larger the surface area of your container, the faster your meals can cool to room temperature for refrigerating and freezing, so choose containers that are low and wide rather than high and narrow, if space allows. If you haven't got any containers, work out how much space you have in your freezer and then look for the most appropriately-sized storage containers that will fit the available space.

Glass

Glass storage containers are great for storing Foodbanked meals in your freezer, as well as keeping herbs and leafy greens fresh. Glass storage containers are also preferable to plastic containers, which often contain harmful BPAs that can leach into your food when it is defrosted or reheated. With glass containers, you can use the same container to defrost the meal in the microwave (if you have one) and wash it easily in the dishwasher afterwards.

Plastic

Plastic storage containers are highly versatile. Look for BPA-free ones if possible. Check to see if they are microwave-safe, if not, simply leave the food to defrost in your fridge and reheat the meals in a saucepan.

Freezable Snap-lock Bags

If you are short on space, freezable snap-lock bags that you can write on are a good solution. We like to write the date cooked, the meal and the number of serves on the bags for easy reference. You can squeeze out the air, close them tightly and store them flat, which will maximise the space in your freezer. Packed this way, meals are also quick to defrost.

Silicone Storage Bags

Recently we've been using silicone food storage bags for our Foodbanked meals. They are great space savers, they don't leak and they can go in the dishwasher. They can also be reused over and over again, unlike snap-lock bags which have a limited life.

Lighten the Load

Having a helping hand – whether it is with shopping, cooking a meal or two, the lunchbox baking, ordering the groceries online or stacking the dishwasher after dinner every night – will lighten the load.

WAYS SOME HOUSEHOLDS DIVIDE TASKS

	Family of 2 adults, young kids	Family of 2 adults, tweens or teens and a young kid	Family of 2 adults, and 2 tweens or teens	Single parent family with tweens and young kids
Adult 1	• Shop • Cook weeknights	• Cook weeknights	• Cook 4 nights	• Cook 4 nights
Adult 2	• Cook weekends	• Shop • Cook weekends	• Shop • Serve 2 Foodbanked meals	N/A
Teens or tweens	N/A	• Bake lunchbox snacks	• Cook 1 meal (Super Simple or Fast & Fresh) • Bake lunchbox snacks	• Help order online groceries • Cook 1 night each
Old enough to help	• Set and clear the table	• Stack and unstack the dishwasher	• Make pancakes or cook eggs	• Bake lunchbox snacks • Reheat food on Super Simple leftovers night

So, if you are in a household of more than one, work out how to carve a few food-related tasks off your to-do list by sharing the load.

> Encourage kids to get involved in cooking: upskill them as they grow.

SHOP ONLINE

Online shopping is made for busy people, particularly for parents of young kids. Spend a few minutes setting up a regular online order and getting used to the system, then get someone else to trawl the aisles for you and deliver your groceries to your door, or order online and collect your shopping at your convenience.

KIDS IN THE KITCHEN

Teaching your kids some kitchen basics is a great way to build life skills. Sometimes, we are tempted to start them on the boring tasks like peeling potatoes and chopping onions, which – surprise, surprise – doesn't get them inspired and generally makes them cry. So, start them early with some fun baking, then gradually introduce everyday cooking skills. Simple weekend breakfasts like pancakes, French toast or eggs are great starting points, and you can move up to easy dinner meals as the kids get older.

TASKS THAT GROW AS THEY GROW

YOUNG KIDS
- Setting and clearing the table
- Helping choose the week's meals
- Stacking and unstacking the dishwasher
- Washing and drying up
- Helping put the shopping away
- Baking lunchbox snacks
- Making sandwiches
- Assembling lunchboxes

TWEENS
- Toasting sandwiches
- Learning to cook eggs (scrambled, fried, boiled, working up to poached)
- Making pancakes or cooking Sunday breakfast
- Mastering more Super Simple meals like jacket potatoes, flatbread pizzas, BLTs

EARLY ADULTS
- Reheating Foodbanked Double-Up meals and making Speedy Sides
- Cooking basics like chopping an onion
- Cooking Fast & Fresh meals
- Helping with the shopping list, online ordering, etc.
- Cooking Double-Up meals
- Helping with food budgeting

SUNDAY 12 MAY
SHEPHERD'S PIE

MONDAY 13 MAY
CHICK PEA CURRY

TUESDAY 14 MAY
BEAN & BARLEY
BRAISE

WEDNESDAY 15 MAY
NAPOLITANA
PASTA SAUCE

THURSDAY 16 MAY
Drag your
recipe here.

FRIDAY 17 MAY
Drag your
recipe here.

Dining Out

CHICKEN & CHORIZO BRAISE

Frozen

TABOULI

CHICKEN PIE WITH PUFF TOPPING

Plan

How to Get Started in 10 Easy Steps

Great, I'm in, you say. But how do I get started?
Here's our guide to making meal planning simple.

1. Think about cooking as something easy rather than a chore. Don't worry about waiting for inspiration on what to cook. Taking a 'just get it done' mindset will make everyday dinner cooking an easy part of each day.

2. Look at your weekly schedule and work out when you have crazy busy nights and when you have more time to cook. Match meals to your schedule. Things tend to change every few months, so keep a planner on hand to cross-check your busy times. See our template on page 38.

3. Make sure you have some pots that are large enough to cook your Double-Up meals and ensure you have all the necessary kitchen tools – see our list on pages 62–3.

4. Ask other family members for their ideas on what they'd like to eat, but also plan to introduce new dishes regularly to expand your options.

5. Plan on using the ingredients you already have and need to use up. This will save money and cut down on shopping time.

6. Choose meals that are easy to cook. Keep your Masterchef aspirations for visitors or dinner parties – everyday meals should be tasty but simple to make.

7. Get a good selection of pantry and fridge staples, such as Asian sauces, pasta, some tinned or dried legumes and olive oil.

8. Make your meal plan and shopping list. See our templates on pages 48 and 49, or try the PlanBuyCook app, which automatically generates your shopping list and allows you to easily double up quantities on meals.

9. Get some meals in the freezer while you are reading this book, so you can get into the swing of the 4+2+1 mode as soon as possible. For example, start by making a Tasty Bolognese Sauce (page 83) and the Bean Quesadillas mix (page 137) – both doubled – so you can take two Foodbanked meals out of the freezer by week two.

10. Relax and enjoy cooking again – once it is no longer painful, you will get dinner done in a no-fuss, routine way that will allow you more time to enjoy other things.

Planning Your 4+2+1 Schedule

Matching meals to your schedule is key to cutting down your weekday cooking time.

I start by looking at which activities I need to be involved with. I ignore anything after school that doesn't require parental involvement or transport of children.

Opposite is a simplified version of my week to show you how I work out which nights are good for Double-Up, Fast & Fresh, Foodbanked or Super Simple meals.

If your family is anything like mine, and your partner gets home from work at 6.30 pm at the earliest, it is pretty realistic to only expect help with the weekend cooking or shopping.

Cooking the two Double-Up meals on Sunday gets me ahead for the rest of the week.

Whatever day I do the shopping, I make that night a Super Simple or Foodbank meal night – food shopping takes some time and I don't fancy thinking about food much once we've put it all away.

Now it's your turn. Add your own commitments to the schedule on page 38: exercise, music, time home from work, then write down your children's activities (if you have them) to see how you can match your 4+2+1 meal plan with your schedule.

Meals to add:

Double-Up meal #1 and #2

Fast & Fresh meal #1 and #2

2 × Foodbanked meals

1 × Super Simple meal

Remember to also note when the food shopping will be done.

If you are busy every night from Monday to Friday, plan to cook two meals at once on the weekend – either two Double-Up meals, or one Double-Up meal and one Fast & Fresh to save time during the week.

GABY'S SAMPLE SCHEDULE

	Adults	Kids	4+2+1 time
Sunday			Cook two Double-Up meals. Freeze one of each. Eat Double-Up #1
Monday	Work from home	Child 3: Sport drop off 4.30 pm	Fast & Fresh #1
Tuesday	Work – home at 5 pm	Child 3: Swimming pick-up 6 pm	Eat Double-Up #2
Wednesday	Work – home at 6 pm	Child 2: Training pick-up 7 pm Child 1: Training pick-up 8 pm	Foodbanked meal from freezer
Thursday	Work – home at 5 pm	All 3 children: Basketball training	Foodbanked meal from freezer
Friday	Work from home (plus food shopping)		Super Simple meal
Saturday	Taking kids to sport	Sport, sport and more sport	Fast & Fresh #2

Your Schedule

	Adults	Kids	4+2+1 time
Sunday			
Monday			
Tuesday			
Wednesday			
Thursday			
Friday			
Saturday			

Download this template and print at home:

planbuycook.com.au/templates

Choosing Your Weekly Meals

When thinking about choosing a week's worth of meals with the 4+2+1 formula, Jen and I like to start with a few basic principles.

- Choose two Double-Up meals per week – double the ingredients for these meals on your shopping list. (The PlanBuyCook app can do this easily for you.)
- Choose two Fast & Fresh meals.
- Write down which two Foodbanked meals you will be taking from the freezer this week.
- Remember to add your Super Simple meal to your plan.
- Plan at least one vegetarian meal each week. We all need to increase our vegetable intake, and vegetarian food is also a great way to cut down the cost of your shopping by saving money on meat.
- Mix up the protein offering to include lamb, chicken, beef, pork and fish.
- Variety is the spice of life. Mix up the cuisines and plan, for example, one pasta meal and one rice-based meal each week.
- For families with kids, it is good to have some meals on the list you know your children will like, as well as at least one 'stretch' meal – a meal that is outside of your standard repertoire to introduce new tastes or textures.

- Plan the main component of the meal first, which might be the marinated meat, the pasta sauce or a braise, then add the Speedy Sides once you have firmed-up the 4+2+1 plan.
- On the following pages, we've simplified the process by including a month's worth of meal plans for each season to give you an idea of how the 4+2+1 formula can work, and how to plan your cooking week to minimise time spent cooking during the working week.
- If you regularly have a meal out, eat takeaway or are planning to have a leftovers night each week *as well as* making a Super Simple meal, you can cut down your Fast & Fresh meals to one meal per week – genius! Remember, always make two Double-Up meals each week to keep your Foodbank well stocked.

Summer Meal Plan

If you are starting your 4+2+1 program from scratch in summer, get cracking the week before (week 0) and double:

- Hamburgers (page 88)
- Bean Quesadillas (page 137)

Eat one meal of each that week and freeze the rest for Week 2.

	WEEK 1	WEEK 2
Double-Up	Lamb Kibbeh	Tacos
Double-Up	Greek Pork Skewers	Indian Chicken Marinade
Fast & Fresh	Udon Noodles	Fettuccine Carbonara
Fast & Fresh	Thai Beef Salad	Vegetable Stir-fry
Foodbank	Fish with Salsa Verde*	Bean Quesadillas
Foodbank	San Choy Bau*	Hamburgers
Super Simple	Sausages and Mash or leftovers	Omelette or leftovers

* If starting from scratch in summer, you need to cook an extra two Fast & Fresh meals in Week 1 because you may not have Foodbanked meals yet.

	WEEK 3	WEEK 4
Double-Up	Mango Chicken	Lemongrass Beef Marinade
Double-Up	Chilli con Carne	Barbecue Lamb with Couscous
Fast & Fresh	Fish Cakes	Pesto
Fast & Fresh	Puttanesca Sauce	Stir-fried Mince with XO Sauce
Foodbank	Lamb Kibbeh	Tacos
Foodbank	Greek Pork Skewers	Indian Chicken Marinade
Super Simple	Toasted Sandwiches or leftovers	Steak Sandwiches or leftovers

Greyed-out meals only require minimal cooking time or reheating plus sides (for Foodbanked meals).

Plan Buy Cook

HOW TO COOK THE SAMPLE SUMMER MEAL PLAN – WEEK 2

Saturday: Shopping, Double-Up + Foodbank

Marinate a double portion of meat in Indian Chicken Marinade. Put half in the fridge for Monday and freeze the other half.

Hamburgers. Cook the Foodbanked burger patties and assemble the burgers for dinner.

Cooking time: 20 minutes

Sunday: Double-Up

Make the Taco meat mix (doubled) and prep salads to accompany the tacos. Split the meat mix in half. Eat half for dinner and freeze the other half.

Cooking time: 1 hour

Monday: Double-Up (already marinated)

Indian Chicken. Marinated on Saturday. Cook the meat on the barbecue. Make salads.

Cooking time: 30 minutes

Tuesday: Fast & Fresh

Fettuccine Carbonara, cooked from scratch.

Cooking time: 15 minutes

Wednesday: Fast & Fresh

Vegetable Stir-fry, cooked from scratch.

Cooking time: 30 minutes

Thursday: Foodbank

Bean Quesadillas. Reheat the frozen bean mixture, make fresh salsa, assemble and cook the quesadillas.

Cooking time: 20 minutes

Friday: Super Simple

Omelette. Make omelettes including the filling.

Cooking time: 20 minutes

Total cooking time: 3½ hours
Weekday cooking time: 2 hours

Autumn Meal Plan

If you are starting your 4+2+1 program from scratch in autumn, get cracking the week before (week 0) and double:

- Lamb Tagine (page 101)
- Vegetable Lasagne (page 109)

Eat one meal of each that week and freeze the rest for Week 2.

	WEEK 1	WEEK 2
Double-Up	Falafel Fritters	Five-spice Marinade
Double-Up	Lamb Fricassée	Chickpea Curry
Fast & Fresh	Fried Rice	Spanakopita
Fast & Fresh	Pastitsio	Pad Thai
Foodbank	Niçoise Salad*	Lamb Tagine
Foodbank	Minestrone*	Vegetable Lasagne
Super Simple	Eggs on Toast or leftovers	Toasted Sandwiches or leftovers

* If starting from scratch in autumn, you need to cook an extra two Fast & Fresh meals in Week 1 because you may not have Foodbanked meals yet.

	WEEK 3	WEEK 4
Double-Up	Chicken & Chorizo Braise	Chicken & Lemon Tagine
Double-Up	Middle Eastern Meatballs	Split Pea Dahl
Fast & Fresh	Chicken Yakitori	Pantry Tuna Pasta
Fast & Fresh	Fried Vermicelli Noodles	Portuguese Butterflied Chicken
Foodbank	Lamb Fricassée	Chickpea Curry
Foodbank	Falafel Fritters	Five-spice Marinade and salad
Super Simple	Jacket Potatoes or leftovers	BLTs or leftovers

Greyed-out meals only require minimal cooking time or reheating plus sides (for Foodbanked meals).

HOW TO COOK THE SAMPLE AUTUMN MEAL PLAN – WEEK 2

Saturday: Shopping, Double-Up + Foodbank

Marinate a double portion of meat for the Five-spice Marinade. Refrigerate half for Monday and freeze the other half.

Reheat/cook the Vegetable Lasagne and make a leafy green salad for dinner.

Cooking time: 40 minutes

Sunday: Double-Up + Fast & Fresh

Cook a double portion of Chickpea Curry, refrigerate half for Tuesday and freeze the other half. Make Spanakopita from scratch and serve with a side salad for dinner.

Cooking time: 90 minutes

Monday: Double-Up (already marinated)

Cook the Five-spice Marinade meat with a side of Asian Greens.

Cooking time: 20 minutes

Tuesday: Double-Up (already made)

Heat the Chickpea Curry and steam some rice as a side.

Cooking time: 20 minutes

Wednesday: Foodbank

Reheat the defrosted Lamb Tagine. Cook couscous and steam some veg.

Cooking time: 20 minutes

Thursday: Fast & Fresh

Pad Thai, cooked from scratch.

Cooking time: 40 minutes

Friday: Super Simple

Leftovers. Reheat and serve.

Cooking time: 10 minutes

Total cooking time: 4 hours
Weekday cooking time: 1 hour 50 minutes

Winter Meal Plan

If you are starting your 4+2+1 program from scratch in winter, get cracking the week before (week 0) and double:

- Tasty Bolognese Sauce (page 83)
- Middle Eastern Meatballs (page 102)

Eat one meal of each that week and freeze the rest for Week 2.

	WEEK 1	WEEK 2
Double-Up	Chicken Pie with Potato Topping	Chicken Pasta Sauce
Double-Up	Bean & Barley Braise	Lamb Curry
Fast & Fresh	Thai Pork Stir-fry	Tex-mex Rice with Corn
Fast & Fresh	Linda's Chicken Gumbo	Chicken Hokkien Noodles
Foodbank	Steak Sandwich*	Middle Eastern Meatballs
Foodbank	Fish with Salsa Verde*	Lasagne (using frozen Tasty Bolognese Sauce)
Super Simple	Eggs on Toast or leftovers	Toasted Sandwiches or leftovers

* If starting from scratch in winter, you need to cook an extra two Fast & Fresh meals in Week 1 because you may not have Foodbanked meals yet.

	WEEK 3	WEEK 4
Double-Up	Chilli con Carne	Italian Meatballs
Double-Up	Beef Stroganoff	Lamb Kibbeh
Fast & Fresh	Puttanesca Sauce	Pesto
Fast & Fresh	Udon Noodles	Pad Thai
Foodbank	Bean & Barley Braise	Lamb Curry
Foodbank	Chicken Pie with Potato Topping	Chicken Pasta Sauce
Super Simple	Flatbread Pizzas or leftovers	Jacket Potatoes or leftovers

Greyed-out meals only require minimal cooking time or reheating plus sides (for Foodbanked meals).

Plan Buy Cook

HOW TO COOK THE SAMPLE WINTER MEAL PLAN – WEEK 2

Saturday: Shopping + Fast & Fresh

Cook the Chicken Hokkien Noodles from scratch.

Cooking time: 30 minutes

Sunday: Double-Up

Cook a double portion of Chicken Pasta Sauce, put half in the fridge for Wednesday and freeze the other half. Cook a double portion of Lamb Curry and steam some rice. Eat half that night. Freeze the other half.

Cooking time: 2.5 hours

Monday: Fast & Fresh

Cook the Tex-mex Rice with Corn from scratch.

Cooking time: 40 minutes

Tuesday: Foodbank

Take the Tasty Bolognese mix from the freezer and reheat. Make the béchamel sauce, assemble the Lasagne, and bake in the oven.

Cooking time: 50 minutes

Wednesday: Double-Up (already done)

Heat the Chicken Pasta Sauce and cook pasta.

Cooking time: 10 minutes

Thursday: Foodbank

Take the Middle Eastern Meatballs from the freezer, reheat and serve with bread.

Cooking time: 10 minutes

Friday: Super Simple

Make some Toasted Sandwiches.

Cooking time: 10 minutes

Total cooking time: 5 hours
Weekday cooking time: 2 hours

Spring Meal Plan

If you are starting your 4+2+1 program from scratch in spring, get cracking the week before (week 0) and double:

- Easy Asian Skewers (page 125)
- Chicken & Chorizo Braise (page 71)

Eat one meal of each that week and freeze the rest for Week 2.

	WEEK 1	WEEK 2
Double-Up	Shepherd's Pie	Tasty Bolognese Sauce
Double-Up	Indian Chicken Marinade	Baked Beans
Fast & Fresh	Haloumi & Pumpkin Fritters	Eggplant Wraps
Fast & Fresh	Crumbed Chicken Thighs	Vietnamese Chicken Salad
Foodbank	Fried Rice*	Easy Asian Skewers
Foodbank	Pantry Tuna Pasta*	Chicken & Chorizo Braise
Super Simple	BLTs or leftovers	Toasted Sandwiches or leftovers

* If starting from scratch in spring, you need to cook an extra two Fast & Fresh meals in Week 1 because you may not have Foodbanked meals yet.

	WEEK 3	WEEK 4
Double-Up	Five-spice Marinade	Italian Sausage & White Bean Braise
Double-Up	Chicken & Lemon Tagine	Grecian Beef
Fast & Fresh	Fish Cakes	Poached Chicken & Lamb with Rice
Fast & Fresh	Fried Vermicelli Noodles	Asian Beef Mince
Foodbank	Shepherd's Pie	Baked Beans
Foodbank	Indian Chicken Marinade (wraps)	Tasty Bolognese Sauce or Lasagne (using Tasty Bolognese Sauce)
Super Simple	Eggs on Toast or leftovers	Flatbread Pizzas or leftovers

Greyed-out meals only require minimal cooking time or reheating plus sides (for Foodbanked meals).

HOW TO COOK THE SAMPLE SPRING MEAL PLAN – WEEK 2

Saturday: Shopping + Fast & Fresh

Vietnamese Chicken Salad. Make from scratch (or cheat with a store-bought chook). Add steamed rice on the side.

Cooking time: 35 minutes

Sunday: Double-Up

Cook Tasty Bolognese Sauce and Baked Beans (doubled). Eat half the Bolognese with pasta, freeze the other half. Refrigerate half the Baked Bean mix for Wednesday and freeze the other half.

Cooking time: 90 minutes

Monday: Fast & Fresh

Make Eggplant Wraps from scratch.

Cooking time: 40 minutes

Tuesday: Foodbank

Reheat the Chicken & Chorizo Braise, steam veg as a side.

Cooking time: 20 minutes

Wednesday: Double-Up (already done)

Reheat the Baked Bean mix and make toast.

Cooking time: 10 minutes

Thursday: Foodbank

Cook Easy Asian Skewers on the barbecue, make two salads.

Cooking time: 30 minutes

Friday: Super Simple

BLATs: Cook bacon, slice tomatoes, prep salad and avocado and assemble the sandwiches.

Cooking time: 15 minutes

Total cooking time: 4 hours
Weekday cooking time: 2 hours

Weekly Planner Template

Download these templates and print them at home:

planbuycook.com.au/templates

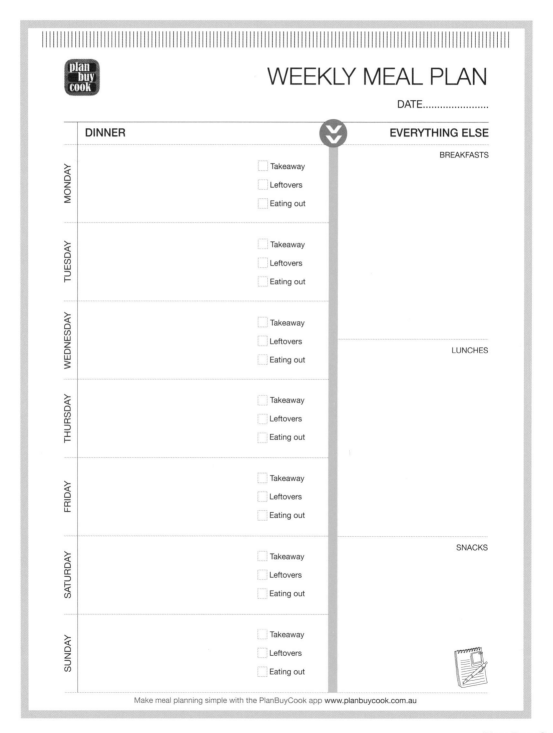

Shopping List Template

SHOPPING LIST

FRUIT & VEGETABLES

MEAT & FISH

FRIDGE, FREEZER & DELI

PANTRY & BAKERY

HOUSEHOLD

NOTES

The PlanBuyCook app automatically generates your shopping list www.planbuycook.com.au

Buy

Food is a large-ticket item in the family budget, and it's only getting bigger. Apart from mortgage or rent, it is the biggest household expense for most families. So how can you save money on your food bills?

As a rule of thumb, cooking from scratch will save you in the short and long term. It's better for the budget and for your health. Have a good repertoire of everyday meals made from ingredients you recognise so you don't reach for too many takeaways, expensive pre-made food from the supermarket or end up dining out due to lack of ingredients. Your 4+2+1 meal plan is the key to ensuring you have the ingredients at home to cook great meals from scratch.

Having a list will stop some of the impulse purchases that shops are willing you to make. We have included a checklist of what to do before, during and after shopping to help you with shopping day (see opposite page).

There are also great ways to save on your everyday food items, which we have highlighted in Small Swaps on page 54.

Meal boxes have become popular too, so we've done some of the sums for you to compare the cost of the average meal box for a family of four with the cost of all the ingredients if you shop for them yourself (see page 56). And we look at when to order takeaway versus when to cook at home (page 57).

Having some core cooking staples in the pantry and fridge, as well as some great pots and utensils to cook with, will make your everyday cooking a breeze. See our list of staples (pages 58–61) and our kitchen essentials (pages 62–63) to get you on track.

To the Shops We Go …

MAKING YOUR PLAN

☐ Use the 4+2+1 formula to plan your meals.

BEFORE YOU SHOP

☐ Check the fridge for ingredients you need to use up or can substitute for ingredients you need this week. Check your pantry and fridge for sides such as pasta, rice or fresh vegetables and salad.

☐ Make your shopping list, taking into account what you already have at home. Remember to double all the ingredients for your two Double-Up meals.

☐ Don't forget vegetables and salad, breakfast items, lunch ingredients and snacks.

See our shopping list template on page 49.

☐ Remember your shopping bags.

☐ Eat something – when you are hungry you tend to buy more food than you need. True story.

HOME FROM SHOPPING

☐ Marinate meat straight away. Freeze half and store the other half in the fridge ready for cooking during the week.

☐ Wash, spin and store your fresh herbs – they will last all week (see page 27).

☐ Wash the fruit and put it into the fruit bowl, ready to eat.

☐ Make shopping night a Fast & Fresh or Super Simple meal night. Tackle the cooking in bulk and the lunchbox snacks another day.

TAKING KIDS TO THE SUPERMARKET? OUR SURVIVAL TIPS

- Go with a list. Once kids can read, get them to see whether items are on the list e.g. chocolate: no, eggs: yes.

- Grab a piece of fruit for them to eat while shopping.

- Talk about special occasion foods vs everyday foods at checkout.

- Play 'guess the amount' at the checkout.

Small Swaps for Big Savings

We are all looking to save money at the checkout without compromising on the food we eat. Here are some small changes that can have a big impact on your weekly family food budget.

USE CHEAPER CUTS OF MEAT

Having some great recipes that use beef shin (often labelled as 'gravy beef'), pork neck (often labelled pork scotch) or chuck steak rather than eye fillet and other expensive cuts can make meat more affordable. These cheaper cuts generally require longer cooking, but they have great flavour. For meat at a lower cost, look for tasty meals that use minced chicken, turkey, pork, lamb, veal or beef. Supermarkets are practically giving away chicken drumsticks now, so think about ways to use them too.

CHEESE PLEASE

Block cheese is the cheapest way to get your fill of cheddar. While we can now buy it sliced, grated or as individually packed cheese sticks, you can save about $5 a kilo (at least) by buying it as a block and doing the slicing, cutting and grating yourself. Get the kids used to blocks or batons of cheese in their lunchbox, rather than packaged cheese sticks. Saves on packaging too.

FLAVOURED OR SQUEEZY YOGHURT

Make your own flavoured yoghurt by buying plain or Greek yoghurt in bulk and mixing it with vanilla and a bit of icing sugar, grated apple and cinnamon, or simply purée any frozen berries, mango or banana you already have in the freezer. Kids can choose their favourite flavours, and you control the ingredients. Or learn to love plain or Greek yoghurt – it is so versatile, goes with many meals and can double as a snack.

UGLY VEGETABLES

You can save on fresh vegetables by choosing the less glamorous ones on sale. They taste the same but may not look as perfect as the full-priced equivalent. Overripe bananas for smoothies and banana bread are often discounted substantially. Grab them while you can. You can always freeze what you do not need immediately for later use.

WHOLEGRAIN CEREAL

There is so much more value in wholegrain breakfast cereal than flavoured cereal. You get twice the amount of cereal in a standard family-sized box for about a third of the cost by weight of its sweetened counterparts. Wholegrain cereal is also healthier and more filling, so the kids (and other family members) will last longer without the need for more food.

MAKE YOUR OWN MARINADES

Buying meat that has already been marinated is more expensive than buying plain meat. If you make your own simple marinades, you can save money and control the sugar and salt content yourself. Most of our homemade marinade recipes only have a few ingredients, but they are still loaded with flavour.

SWAP IN A VEGETARIAN FOOD

Cutting meat out of at least one meal a week is a sure-fire way to save. Try Bean Quesadillas (page 137), Vegetable Lasagne (page 109), Chickpea Curry (page 138) or our Vegetable Stir-fry (page 167). The key is to ensure the meal is tasty and filling enough so that the kids don't miss the meat on the plate.

HOMEMADE MUESLI BARS AND SNACKS

Rolled oats are so cheap they are almost free, so whipping up your own muesli bars with a few simple ingredients is a great way to save money and reduce food packaging. Same goes for most snack foods in the lunchbox – they are generally way cheaper to make than buy, and can be frozen in bulk.

HOME BRANDS

Your supermarket's home brand is a good alternative for saving on standard items such as flour, sugar and other pantry staples. Try out each product first in small amounts to ensure it doesn't affect the taste or your cooking. The difference to your savings can really add up over the course of the year.

JUICE AND SOFT DRINKS

Lose the juice from the weekly shop. It is expensive and full of sugar without much fibre. Soft drinks may be cheap but, again, are no good for you or your teeth. Save them for special occasions. Stick to milk and water (it's free) and eat whole fruit. Your teeth and your sugar levels will thank you.

BUY IN BULK

Buying certain pantry staples (such as oils and sauces) in bulk can save money – compare prices between smaller bottles of olive oil and large metal canisters, for example.

The savings are in the bank.

Meal Boxes vs 4+2+1 Cooking: Counting the Costs

The rising popularity of meal boxes is simply astounding. Meal boxes can be reasonably cost effective for couples, but once you start ordering them for your family, you will notice they can be quite expensive.

We did a price comparison between the average cost of a meal box from the market leaders for a family of four for four meals, and the cost of the ingredients for four similar PlanBuyCook meals. In Australia, the average cost of a meal box with four meals (and lots of packaging) for a family of four is $120.

We costed out the ingredients – including the cost of oil, spices and condiments used – for four meals in our Cook section (page 65) using a variety of meals.

Wait for it: the difference was $57 with just four meals. It is so much cheaper to plan and shop for your own meals. You could get the ingredients for the extra three dinners that week – yes seven meals for four people – plus some extra shopping for less than the cost of the four meals for four people meal box.

Plus, even if you did use a meal box, you would still need to go to the supermarket for bread, milk, eggs and cereal as a minimum, let alone fruit, lunches and snacks for the week, and household items such as cleaning products. There is also that pesky matter of the other three meals you need to eat that week that don't come with your meal box.

Some of the appeal of meal boxes is outsourcing the thinking about what meals you are going to make. That's when the 4+2+1 routine really comes into its own. You get to choose your own recipes, and you make extra for future weeks.

Ditch the meal box idea and make your own plan, then use the savings for a holiday. Done.

 You can use the PlanBuyCook app to auto-generate your shopping list for families of any size.

PlanBuyCook Meals	Bean & Barley Braise	Hamburgers	Chicken Pie with Potato Topping	Lamb Curry
Veg	$1.50	$3.80	$4.50	$4.10
Meat	N/A	$6.50	$8.50	$19.00
Condiments	$0.80	$1.00	$0.35	$3.35
Other	$6.00 (beans, etc.)	$3.60 (rolls, cheese, etc.)		
Total (4 serves)	**$8.30**	**$14.90**	**$13.35**	**$26.45**

TOTAL: $63 FOR 4 MEALS

To Takeaway or Not?

For many families, takeaway is a weekly habit. Takeaway is a great option if you fancy a particular cuisine. And, in general, one takeaway meal a week is not too bad for your diet either. As one dietitian told us, if twenty of your twenty-one breakfasts, lunches and dinners each week are pretty healthy, don't beat yourself up over one meal of fish and chips if that's what you feel like.

Takeaway is not so great when it is eaten twice a week, or because you haven't got any other options. It is also not so great if your family members are regularly having fast-food lunches or other meals. Teenagers, we are looking at you here …

Before I started meal planning, my family would have takeaway weekly (or more often) because I couldn't think of what to eat that night or didn't have the ingredients at home to cook a full meal. Now that I know what we are eating, and I have some great Fast & Fresh recipes in my repertoire and Foodbanked meals in the freezer, I only use takeaway if we really want a particular food.

I quickly worked out that at $50 plus per meal for my family of five, the cost of takeaway was also very high for a single meal, relative to cooking at home. That's $2600 a year in takeaway food – meals I didn't particularly enjoy, but that were convenient.

You may also need to get over the idea that your kids prefer a takeaway meal to your home cooking. I used to find it a little offensive when I asked one of my kids what he'd like for dinner and his top selections would be takeaway, but now I just laugh it off. I think many kids like the immediacy of a takeaway meal rather than waiting and watching you cook at home – growing kids are often hungry.

A Foodbanked meal is the ultimate fast food anyway – way faster than ordering takeaway or waiting for home delivery, and better for our health and our bank balance.

So, use takeaway as a meal of choice when you really want to eat a particular food that tastes better from a shop rather than from home.

And if you have a regular takeaway meal, plan for it as well so you don't waste fresh food.

 You can plan a takeaway meal as your Super Simple meal so you don't buy extra food each week that will go to waste.

A Foodbanked meal from your freezer is faster than a takeaway meal.

Pantry Staples

Stock up on these basics to make cooking your everyday meals easy. Jen and I have each checked our pantries and fridges, plus all the recipes in the Cook section (page 65) to find the most popular ingredients.

General

Jasmine rice

Arborio rice

Couscous

Pasta of your choice

Tortillas and tacos

Coarse cracked (bulgur) wheat

Lentils

Red kidney beans

Chickpeas

Cannellini (lima) beans

Tinned corn

Capers

Anchovies in oil

Pitted kalamata olives

Tuna in oil

Chicken and/or vegetable stock

Tinned diced tomatoes – you can never have enough of these!

Tomato passata (puréed tomatoes)

Tomato paste (concentrated purée)

Red curry paste

Onions

Shallots

Crispy fried shallots

Garlic

Potatoes

Cashew nuts

Peanuts

Currants

Oils, Vinegars, Sauces and Condiments

Olive oil

Sesame oil

White balsamic vinegar

Balsamic vinegar

White vinegar

Rice vinegar

Tomato sauce (ketchup)

Worcestershire sauce

Light soy sauce

Sweet soy sauce (kecap manis)

Mirin (Japanese rice wine)

Shaoxing (Chinese rice wine)

Fish sauce

Oyster sauce

Hoisin sauce

Sriracha (hot chilli sauce)

Sweet chilli sauce

Sambal oelek

Dijon mustard

Mango chutney

DID YOU KNOW?

Some chicken stock cubes are vegan – they are 'chicken style', so suitable for vegetarian/vegan cooking.

Spices and Dried Herbs

Iodised salt

Sea salt flakes

Black pepper

White pepper

Bay leaves

Ground cinnamon

Garam masala

Ground turmeric

Ground ginger

Ground coriander

Ground cumin

Dried chilli flakes

Dried Greek oregano (on the stem)

A WORD ABOUT OILS AND BUTTER

We realised that we don't actually need loads of different oils in the pantry.

Our simple solution? **Olive oil**.

Standard olive oil is a great all-round cooking option that we use in our kitchens for everything from frying and wok cooking to baking.

Now, when we say olive oil we don't mean first-pressed, extra-virgin olive oil. This is a great oil, but we mainly use it for salad dressings as it is packed with flavour and can change the taste of your dishes. We tend to keep extra-virgin olive oil in smaller quantities for this reason.

Buy your stock-standard olive oil in bulk and decant it into smaller containers in your kitchen.

We also use sesame oil for flavour in Asian cooking and butter as an alternative for cooking eggs and some baking, as well as using it as our daily spread option.

We have eliminated cooking spray from our cooking, as we found it damaged the surface of non-stick pans and muffin tins.

Refrigerator and Freezer Staples

FRIDGE

Plain or Greek yoghurt

Block cheese

Parmesan (a block is good and lasts longer)

Feta (stores for longer if you buy it in brine)

Eggs

Milk

Unsalted butter (good for use as a spread and for baking)

Olives

Sliced pickled jalapeño chillies

Mayonnaise

Fresh ginger

FREEZER

Frozen peas

Frozen corn

Frozen spinach

Fish in portions – for a Fast & Fresh meal served with salsa verde

Sausages

Fresh ingredients rescued before going to waste

Home-baked goodies such as slices, muffins and cakes that are already cut into portions, ready for lunchboxes

And, of course, Foodbanked meals including marinated meat

SOME GOOD SHORTCUT INGREDIENTS

- Store-bought roast chicken
- Chicken stock powder or cubes
- Harissa
- Hummus
- Tabbouleh from the deli
- Peeled cooked beetroot (beets) from the fruit and veg section
- Tinned legumes
- Tinned tuna and sardines

Buy

The Only Kitchen Utensils You Need

You don't need to buy the best Japanese knives or the latest gadgets. Our simple collection of must-have items is just about all you need to make great everyday meals.

KNIVES

Chef's Knife

A steel-bladed knife that can be sharpened is essential for prepping food. About 22 cm (9 in) in length is perfect.

Serrated Paring Knives

This great all-rounder is perfect for slicing tomatoes and everything else. For around $10, they are a great investment.

Bread Knife

Great for bread and slicing some vegetables, such as tomatoes.

PANS & OVEN DISHES

Large Sauté Pan

Great for browning meats, for braises and ragu. Buy a pan that is wide and shallow, can be transferred from stovetop to oven and has a lid. You'll have it for years, so invest in a good one if you can. A diameter of 32 cm (13 in) and depth of about 10 cm (4 in) works well for Double-Up meals.

Large Saucepan

Great for cooking pasta or larger quantities of freezable meals. Choose a larger diameter, about 26 cm (10¼ in), to make cooking in bulk easy.

Frying Pans

Have a small frying pan, about 20 cm (8 in), for omelettes or scrambled eggs, and a larger one, 28 cm (11 in), for cooking Double-Up meals or other meat when the weather doesn't allow for barbecuing outside.

Wok

A wok is great for Fast & Fresh Asian dishes.

Lasagne Dish

Perfect for baked dishes or for marinating meats.

UTENSILS

Fine Hand-held Grater

This is the tool for grating ginger, garlic or parmesan. It will be used every day, so it's good to find one that will last.

Hand-held Slicer or Mandoline

This is good for shredding or slicing vegetables, such as cabbage and radishes, for coleslaw and salads, or anything requiring a nice even slice.

Julienne Slicer

For super-quick julienned vegetables (matchsticks), mainly for carrots. Makes salad prep easy.

Heatproof Silicone Spatula

Heatproof spatulas are great for baking, scrambled eggs and general cooking.

Sharp Vegetable Peeler

A speed peeler can make peeling vegetables a breeze. It is also great for peeling cucumber and carrots into ribbons for salads. The Swiss brands are often the best.

Digital Thermometer

Really handy for measuring the core temperature of meat or fish. It is especially useful for barbecuing.

Scales

Great for accurately weighing ingredients (especially important when baking).

Cup and Spoon Measures

For ease of measuring most ingredients.

Wok Spatula

This well-shaped tool makes stirring food in your wok a cinch. If you have a steel wok, choose a stainless-steel spatula.

Wooden Spoons

Probably one of the most used items in any kitchen. Have a few on hand to make cooking multiple dishes at once easier.

EQUIPMENT

Salad Spinner

Salad always tastes better when it is spun and dried, as the dressing clings to it nicely. It is good practice to wash all salad leaves regardless of whether they say ready to eat.

Chopping Board

A few thick and heavy chopping boards – wooden or plastic.

PlanBuyCook App (of course!)

Scale your meals to match your household size and double up quantities on all freezable meals. With an auto-generated shopping list and ability to add your own recipes (that the app will scale), it is a perfect meal-planning tool. Available from the App Store: www.appstore.com/planbuycook

Cook

Notes on the Recipes

OVEN TEMPERATURES

All the recipes use fan-forced oven temperatures. If you have a conventional oven, increase the temperature by 20°C (68°F) or half a gas mark.

DIGITAL THERMOMETER

Use a digital thermometer to check the internal temperature of meat or fish. If in doubt, check the internet for temperature guides for meat, which vary according to what cut you're using.

QUANTITIES

Most of our meat recipes use about 150 g (5½ oz) of meat per serve. Round up or down according to the available portions of meat that you buy. For example, if a recipe asks for 600 g (1 lb 5 oz) meat but you can only buy in 500 g (1 lb 2 oz) or 1 kg (2 lb 3 oz) portions, simply use less meat and add more vegetables, or increase the total amount you're making and have leftovers. Teenagers may require slightly larger serves.

COOKING WITH OIL

The recipes use a minimal amount of olive oil. If your vegetables or meat are sticking to the pan, add a splash of water instead of more oil.

SALT AND PEPPER

I use a small amount of salt and cracked black pepper in most recipes to build flavour in the dish. I also recommend adding a small amount of salt when cooking vegetables; they can be very bland, and the flavour is enhanced by using a little salt.

SUGAR

Sugar balances the flavours in Asian sauces and dishes. If you are sugar free, you will need to use your preferred alternative, such as dextrose or rice malt syrup. Taste your dishes to see whether the balance is correct with the replacement.

GLUTEN-FREE (GF)

If you are following a gluten-free diet, it is pretty easy to make most of these recipes using standard gluten-free substitutions. Almost all sauces come with gluten-free alternatives, and the quality of gluten-free pasta, flour and other base ingredients means you can exchange the gluten options with exact quantities of their gluten-free equivalents.

VEGETARIAN (V)

Vegetarian meals are marked with a V throughout the Cook section.

VEGAN (VG)

Vegan recipes are marked with VG throughout the Cook section. Many vegetarian recipes (V) just contain yoghurt, which you can omit to make them vegan (VG).

Jen's Kitchen Time-savers

- When cooking an Asian stir-fry, measure out all the sauces first. It saves you measuring as you go and removes the risk of burning or over-cooking what's on the stove.

- Similarly, for recipes that use a number of ground spices, measure them out before you start, which will speed up your cooking. Great for meals such as curries and tagines.

- Make our Asian salad dressing in bulk (see page 188) to get you through summer. Don't add the garlic and lime juice to your bulk dressing. Instead, measure out the amount you require on the day, then add the garlic and lime to the portion you are serving. This will keep your dressing fresh. Simply add to chicken or Thai Beef Salad (page 186).

- If making Hamburgers (page 88), meatballs (pages 90 and 102) or Falafel Fritters (page 143), you can make the mix 2–3 days in advance and refrigerate, then simply shape and cook on the day.

- Cook grains and roast vegetables for salads to use later in the week. For example, for the Quinoa Salad (page 200), cook the corn and quinoa 1–2 days earlier, then assemble the rest on the night you need it.

- Get lunchbox snacks cooked on the weekend, cut into snack-sized portions, and freeze.

- Cook onion to save some time and store in an airtight container in the fridge for 3–4 days. Cooked onion doesn't smell in your fridge like raw onion. Also, learn how to chop onions like a pro to speed up prep time. YouTube is full of how-to cooking videos.

- If time allows in the morning, prep the dinner's side veggies, like potatoes and carrots, and leave them in water ready to boil that night.

- Use a damp paper towel or cloth underneath your chopping board to stop it from moving around while you chop.

Double-Up Meals

Cook twice as much as you need. Eat one meal this week and freeze the other meal for later. Cook two Double-Up meals each week.

Chicken & Chorizo Braise

This chicken and chorizo braise is a lovely recipe to double and freeze for an extra meal down the track. The chorizo offers a great savoury flavour, eliminating the need for chicken stock. This will become a family favourite for sure.

Prep 20 minutes | Cook 40 minutes | Serves 4

2 tablespoons olive oil

600 g (1 lb 5 oz) boneless chicken thighs, diced

1 red onion, finely diced

1 garlic clove, crushed or grated

250 g (9 oz) chorizo, sliced

2 teaspoons sweet paprika

150 g (5½ oz) store-bought roasted red capsicum (bell pepper), sliced

250 ml (8½ fl oz/1 cup) tomato passata (puréed tomatoes)

125 ml (4 fl oz/½ cup) white wine (optional)

4 flat-leaf (Italian) parsley sprigs, leaves picked, chopped

8 pitted kalamata olives

vegetables (see page 207) or salad, to serve

bread, to serve (optional)

1. Heat half the oil in a saucepan and brown the chicken in batches. Remove from the pan and set aside.

2. Heat the remaining oil in the same pan, then add the onion and garlic with a little water to assist cooking and prevent burning. Cook for 5 minutes.

3. Add the chorizo, paprika and capsicum and cook for 3 minutes.

4. Add the passata, wine (if using) and 300 ml (10½ fl oz) water, then bring to the boil.

5. Return the chicken to the pan. Bring back to the boil and simmer for 20 minutes.

6. Add the parsley and olives and stir to combine. *If doubling up the recipe, split the mixture in two and allow the extra meal to cool to room temperature. Refrigerate overnight before freezing for later use.*

7. Serve with veggies or salad of your choice. Bread is also a great addition.

 If you have a fresh red capsicum (bell pepper) in the fridge, you can use that instead of the roasted capsicum. The roasted capsicum imparts a nice flavour, but use up any fresh capsicum first to avoid food waste.

Chicken & Lemon Tagine

The word 'tagine' refers to both this wonderfully spiced dish and to the vessel that it is traditionally cooked in. This meal is a great introduction to Middle Eastern flavours for children.

Prep 20 minutes | Cook 40 minutes | Serves 4

1 tablespoon olive oil

1 onion, finely diced

2 garlic cloves, crushed or grated

1 carrot, diced

1 celery stalk, diced

¼ teaspoon ground ginger

¼ teaspoon ground turmeric

1 teaspoon ground cumin

1 teaspoon ground coriander

¼ teaspoon ground cinnamon

600 g (1 lb 5 oz) boneless chicken thighs, diced

1 × 400 g (14 oz) tin diced tomatoes

1 × 400 g (14 oz) tin chickpeas, drained and rinsed

1 bay leaf

¼ teaspoon salt

zest of 1 lemon

1 quantity Failsafe Couscous (page 206), to serve

pinch of dried chilli flakes

100 g (3½ oz) plain or Greek yoghurt

fresh coriander (cilantro), to garnish (optional)

1. Heat the olive oil in a saucepan and fry the onion, garlic, carrot and celery. Add a little water (1–2 tablespoons) and cook for 10 minutes.

2. Add the spices and cook for 2 minutes while stirring.

3. Add the chicken and cook until brown.

4. Add the tomatoes and chickpeas, plus enough water to cover the meat, followed by the bay leaf, salt and some pepper.

5. Bring to the boil and simmer for 30 minutes.

6. Add the lemon zest to the tagine and adjust the seasoning if required. *If doubling up the recipe, split the mixture in two and allow the extra meal to cool to room temperature. Refrigerate overnight before freezing for later use.*

7. Cook the couscous according to the recipe on page 206.

8. Sprinkle the tagine with dried chilli flakes and serve with couscous and yoghurt, and garnish with coriander, if desired.

 Green olives or currants make a lovely addition to this dish. You can also add 1 teaspoon honey and some chopped fresh coriander (cilantro) for extra flavour.

Chicken Pie with Potato Topping

This is a great chicken pie without the pastry. You can substitute sweet potato for the white potatoes should you prefer. White pepper has a distinctly different taste to black pepper and gives a great flavour to this pie.

Prep 20 minutes | Cook 50 minutes | Serves 4

6 floury potatoes, peeled and diced

¼ teaspoon salt

2 tablespoons olive oil

1 onion, finely diced

1 garlic clove, crushed

1 carrot, finely diced

1 celery stalk, finely diced

600 g (1 lb 5 oz) boneless chicken thighs, diced

1 bay leaf

1 thyme sprig

2 flat-leaf (Italian) parsley sprigs, leaves picked, chopped

250 ml (8½ fl oz/1 cup) chicken stock

3 tablespoons milk

pinch of ground white pepper

2 tablespoons cornflour (cornstarch)

1. Place the potato and salt in a large saucepan and cover with cold water. Bring to the boil and simmer until the potatoes are soft, about 20 minutes.

2. In a separate large saucepan, heat 1 tablespoon of the oil and fry the onion, garlic, carrot and celery for 10 minutes over a medium heat. Add a little water to stop it sticking.

3. Add the chicken, turn up the heat and brown on all sides.

4. Preheat the oven to 180°C (350°F/Gas Mark 4).

5. Add the bay leaf, thyme, parsley and chicken stock and bring to the boil, then reduce the heat and simmer, uncovered, for 20 minutes. When the chicken is cooked, remove the bay leaf and thyme sprigs and add the milk, white pepper and a pinch of salt.

6. In a little bowl, mix the cornflour with 2 tablespoons water. Bring the chicken mixture back to the boil and add the cornflour mix. Stir continuously for 3 minutes. *If doubling up the recipe, split the mixture in two and allow the extra meal to cool to room temperature. Refrigerate overnight before freezing for later use*. Adjust the seasoning and pour into an ovenproof dish.

7. Drain the potatoes thoroughly, then mash and add the remaining olive oil.

8. Spread the mash on top of the chicken mixture, then place in the oven and cook until golden, about 20 minutes.

 For your Foodbanked meal, once the meat mixture has defrosted, slowly bring it back to the boil while the potatoes cook, and check the seasoning before transferring the mix to the ovenproof dish in step 6.

Chicken Pasta Sauce

This is a variation on my mother-in-law Elda's recipe, which is traditionally made with chicken and veal and served with homemade gnocchi. Veal can be hard to come by unless you have a good Italian butcher, so I have left it out as chicken cooked on the bone adds enough flavour to the dish.

Prep 10 minutes | Cook 1 hour | Serves 4

1 tablespoon olive oil

1 onion, finely diced

1 garlic clove, crushed or grated

1 carrot, finely diced

1 celery stalk, finely diced

2 tablespoons tomato paste (concentrated purée)

6 chicken drumsticks

1 × 400 g (14 oz) tin diced tomatoes

80 ml (2½ fl oz/⅓ cup) white wine (optional)

4 flat-leaf (Italian) parsley sprigs, leaves picked, chopped

1 thyme sprig

1 bay leaf

1 teaspoon salt

400 g (14 oz) pasta of your choice

grated parmesan, to serve

1. Heat the oil in a wide-based saucepan. Add the onion, garlic, carrot and celery and cook over a medium heat for 15 minutes, adding a little water to stop them from browning.

2. Add the tomato paste and cook for a further 2 minutes.

3. Turn up the heat, add the chicken drumsticks and brown on all sides.

4. Add the tomatoes, 80 ml (2½ fl oz/⅓ cup) water, the wine (if using), parsley, thyme, bay leaf, salt and some pepper. Bring to the boil, then reduce the heat and simmer for 40 minutes.

5. Bring a saucepan of salted water to the boil and cook the pasta according to the packet instructions. Strain and set aside.

6. Remove the drumsticks and keep warm. Increase the heat and reduce the sauce for 10 minutes.

7. Remove the bones and skin from the drumsticks, and return the chicken meat to the sauce to heat through. *If doubling up the recipe, split the mixture in two and allow the extra meal to cool to room temperature. Refrigerate overnight before freezing for later use.*

8. Run boiling water over the pasta if needed to reheat it. Divide the pasta between plates then ladle over the sauce. Top with grated parmesan.

 Chicken drumsticks are an economical cut of meat, making this meal budget-friendly.

Chicken Curry

I work with an Indian chef who says no reputable Indian restaurant would ever serve a curry on the day it is made. So cook this on your Double-Up day and store one portion in the fridge for at least a few days before eating to enhance the flavour.

Prep 15 minutes | Cook 1 hour | Serves 4

2 onions, peeled

2 tablespoons olive oil

1 cinnamon stick

2 cardamom pods, lightly bruised

2 whole cloves

600 g (1 lb 5 oz) boneless chicken thighs, diced

1 tablespoon ground cumin

1 tablespoon ground coriander

¼ teaspoon ground turmeric

¼ teaspoon salt

4 tomatoes, diced

1 teaspoon grated fresh ginger

2 garlic cloves, crushed or grated

1 teaspoon garam masala

1 quantity Perfect Steamed Rice (page 205)

100 g (3½ oz/2 cups) baby spinach, washed

plain or Greek yoghurt, to serve

fresh coriander (cilantro), to garnish (optional)

1. Purée the onions in a food processor and set aside.

2. In a large saucepan, heat half the oil, then add the whole spices and cook until fragrant, about 1 minute.

3. Add the chicken and brown on all sides. Remove the spices and chicken from the pan and set aside.

4. Heat the remaining oil in the saucepan, then add the puréed onion. Cook over a medium heat for about 20 minutes, stirring regularly. Add a little water to stop the onion from sticking. It should turn a nice golden colour.

5. Add the ground cumin, coriander, turmeric and salt to the pot, and cook for 5 minutes.

6. Add the tomato and return the chicken and whole spices to the pot. Cover with a lid and simmer for 20 minutes.

7. Add the ginger, garlic and garam masala, and cook for a further 5 minutes.

8. Remove from the heat, leave to cool and store in the fridge. *If doubling up the recipe, split the mixture in two and allow the extra meal to cool to room temperature. Refrigerate overnight before freezing for later use.*

9. On the night you are serving, steam the rice (see page 205, or cook according to the packet instructions). Reheat the curry, stir through the baby spinach and serve with rice and yoghurt. Garnish with fresh coriander, if desired.

 Use a tin of diced tomatoes if you don't have any fresh tomatoes.

Beef Stroganoff

You don't need to break the bank with expensive meat for this classic beef stroganoff. We use beef shin, which is also labelled gravy beef in the supermarket. It is perfect for this slow-cooked dish.

Prep 10 minutes | Cook 2½ hours | Serves 4

3 tablespoons olive oil

3 onions, finely sliced

1¼ teaspoons salt

2 teaspoons white vinegar or 50 ml (1¾ fl oz) white wine

2 teaspoons sweet paprika

1 kg (2 lb 3 oz) beef shin (gravy beef), diced

150 g (5½ oz) button mushrooms, quartered

125 g (4½ oz/½ cup) light sour cream

mashed potato, to serve

steamed greens, to serve

flat-leaf (Italian) parsley, to garnish (optional)

1. Heat 1 tablespoon of the oil in a wide-based, ovenproof saucepan and fry the onions over a low heat for 45 minutes. Stir occasionally and add a little water if the onions begin to stick. You want the onions to melt down, but not colour.

2. Preheat the oven to 150°C (300°F/Gas Mark 2).

3. Add ¼ teaspoon of the salt, the vinegar and the sweet paprika to the onions and cook for 2–3 minutes.

4. Add the beef and cook over a medium heat to seal the meat on all sides.

5. Add 200 ml (7 fl oz) water, then bring to the boil.

6. Place a piece of baking paper on the surface of the meat, then cover the pan with a lid.

7. Cook in the oven for 1½ hours, checking occasionally to make sure it isn't looking dry. Add a little more water if necessary.

8. Meanwhile, heat a non-stick frying pan with the remaining olive oil and cook the mushrooms over a medium heat until golden, then set aside.

9. When the meat is tender, add the mushrooms, sour cream and the remaining salt. *If doubling up the recipe, split the mixture in two and allow the extra meal to cool to room temperature. Refrigerate overnight before freezing for later use.*

10. Serve with mashed potato and steamed greens, or your favourite side, and garnish with parsley, if desired.

Placing a piece of baking paper over the meat (also called a cartouche) keeps the moisture in the dish and prevents evaporation.

Plan Buy Cook

Tasty Bolognese Sauce

Every household needs a favourite recipe for bolognese. Ours uses some bacon to add a little smoky flavour to the sauce. You can use a higher fat beef mince for this recipe instead of veal and pork mince if you prefer.

Prep 10 minutes | Cook 1 hour | Serves 4

1 tablespoon olive oil

2 rashers (slices) bacon, diced

1 onion, finely diced

2 garlic cloves, crushed or grated

1 carrot, finely diced

1 celery stalk, finely diced

500 g (1 lb 2 oz) minced (ground) veal and pork (or pork and beef)

2 tablespoons tomato paste (concentrated purée)

2 × 400 g (14 oz) tins diced tomatoes

1 bay leaf

½ teaspoon salt

pasta of your choice, to serve

grated parmesan, to serve

1. Heat the oil in a large saucepan or cast-iron pan. Add the bacon and cook for 5 minutes.

2. Add the onion, garlic, carrot and celery and cook for 10 minutes. Add a dash of water if the vegetables are browning.

3. Place the meat in the pan and brown, stirring continuously to break up any lumps.

4. Add the tomato paste and stir for 2 minutes to combine.

5. Add the tomatoes, bay leaf and salt. Bring to the boil, then lower the heat and simmer for at least 40 minutes. (The longer you cook the sauce, the better the flavour.)

6. Cook the pasta according to the packet instructions.

7. Serve with parmesan. *If doubling up the recipe, split the sauce in two and allow the extra meal to cool to room temperature. Refrigerate overnight before freezing for later use.*

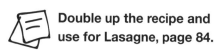 **Double up the recipe and use for Lasagne, page 84.**

Lasagne

Making lasagne is so easy if you have already made the Tasty Bolognese Sauce in advance (see page 83). This allows for a quick assembly of the lasagne on the day you want to eat it, cutting cooking time down to about 45 minutes.

Prep 10 minutes | Cook 1½ hours | Serves 4

1 quantity Tasty Bolognese Sauce (page 83)

500 ml (17 fl oz/2 cups) full-cream (whole) milk

2 tablespoons butter

2 tablespoons plain (all-purpose) flour

¼ teaspoon salt

180 g (7 oz) lasagne sheets

100 g (3½ oz) mozzarella, sliced

50 g (1¾ oz/½ cup) grated parmesan

1. Heat the bolognese sauce before assembling.

2. Make a béchamel sauce by heating the milk in a saucepan until almost boiling.

3. In a separate saucepan, melt the butter, then stir in the flour and cook for 2 minutes, stirring continuously, then add the salt.

4. Gradually add the hot milk to the butter mix a little at a time, using a whisk to incorporate all the milk before adding more. Season to taste. Place a piece of baking paper on the surface of the béchamel and simmer over a low heat for 10 minutes.

5. Preheat the oven to 180°C (350°F/Gas Mark 4).

6. To assemble the lasagne, place one-quarter of the meat sauce in the bottom of a 30 × 20 cm (12 × 8 in) baking dish. Top with a layer of lasagne sheets.

7. Repeat with meat, then sliced mozzarella and lasagne sheets for another two layers.

8. Top with meat sauce, then the béchamel sauce, and then grated parmesan. *If doubling up the recipe, assemble the meals in two dishes. Let the extra lasagne cool down to room temperature, refrigerate overnight and freeze (uncooked) for later use.*

9. Bake for 30 minutes. Once cooked, remove from the oven and leave to stand for 10 minutes before serving.

 Leaving the lasagne to stand for 10 minutes after baking makes it easier to cut.

Chilli con Carne

This is a great dish when there is a crowd to feed. I like to serve it with rice, but my kids love it with corn chips or in wraps. If serving with wraps, cook the meat a little longer to allow excess liquid to absorb, making it easier to eat.

Prep 20 minutes | Cook 1 hour | Serves 4

1 tablespoon olive oil

1 onion, chopped

2 garlic cloves, crushed or grated

3 teaspoons ground cumin

3 teaspoons ground coriander

500 g (1 lb 2 oz) minced (ground) beef

1 green capsicum (bell pepper), finely diced

1 × 400 g (14 oz) tin red kidney beans, drained and rinsed

2 × 400 g (14 oz) tins diced tomatoes

1 teaspoon salt

100 g (3½ oz/½ cup) corn kernels (tinned or frozen)

1 tomato, chopped

4 fresh coriander (cilantro) sprigs, leaves picked, chopped

2 slices pickled jalapeño chilli

1 quantity Perfect Steamed Rice (page 205), corn chips or soft tortillas, to serve

125 g (4½ oz/½ cup) plain or Greek yoghurt, to serve

1. In a large saucepan, heat the oil and fry the onion and garlic.

2. Add 1 tablespoon water to aid cooking and reduce the heat so the onion and garlic don't colour. Cook for 5 minutes, allowing the water to evaporate.

3. Add the cumin and coriander and cook for another 2 minutes.

4. Add the meat and brown, breaking up any lumps as you go, then add the capsicum, kidney beans, 250 ml (8½ fl oz/1 cup) water and the tinned tomatoes.

5. Bring to the boil, add the salt and some pepper and simmer for 50 minutes. *If doubling up the recipe, split the mixture in two and allow the extra meal to cool to room temperature. Refrigerate overnight before freezing for later use.*

6. While the meat is cooking, combine the corn, tomato, fresh coriander and chilli to make a salsa, then set aside.

7. Steam the rice (if using) according to the recipe on page 205, or follow the packet instructions.

8. Serve with steamed rice, corn chips or in tortillas with the yoghurt and salsa.

 Add 1 teaspoon of the pickling liquid from the jalapeños to the chilli; it is a great addition to spice up this dish.

Hamburgers

This is a great hamburger recipe that the whole family will enjoy. Skip the takeaway and whip these up at home. Cooking the onion and garlic improves their flavour.

Prep 10 minutes | Cook 30 minutes | Serves 4

3 tablespoons olive oil

1 onion, finely diced

1 garlic clove, crushed or grated

500 g (1 lb 2 oz) minced (ground) beef

50 g (1¾ oz/½ cup) dry breadcrumbs

2 tablespoons dijon mustard

1 tablespoon worcestershire sauce

4 flat-leaf (Italian) parsley sprigs,
    leaves picked, chopped

1 egg

½ teaspoon salt

4 bread rolls, to serve

4 slices cheese, to serve

sliced tomato, to serve

torn lettuce, to serve

mayonnaise and tomato sauce (ketchup),
    to serve

1. Heat 1 tablespoon olive oil in a small saucepan and cook the onion and garlic over a low heat, but do not brown. Add a little water if the onions begin to stick. Set aside to cool.

2. Combine the meat, breadcrumbs, mustard, worcestershire sauce, parsley, egg, salt and some pepper in a large bowl and mix.

3. Add the cooled onion and garlic mix and use your hands to mix until well combined and sticky.

4. Form the mixture into four patties. *If doubling up the recipe, split the mixture in two, and freeze half for later use.*

5. Heat a barbecue chargrill plate or chargrill pan over a medium–high heat. Add the remaining oil to prevent sticking.

6. Cook the patties for 5 minutes on each side. You may need to lower the heat if they are browning too fast.

7. Remove from the heat and cover with foil while you get ready to build your burgers.

8. Cut each of the bread rolls in half. Assemble the burgers with a patty, sliced cheese, tomato, lettuce, mayonnaise and tomato sauce in whichever order you prefer.

9. Serve immediately.

 Great to make in bulk. Shape the hamburger mix into patties and freeze (raw) in single layers.

Plan Buy Cook

Tacos

Get your Taco Tuesday on this week. Forget the taco kit and make your own taco seasoning and tomato salsa from scratch – it is so easy and preservative- and sugar-free. Just grab some hard or soft tacos and your favourite fillings.

Prep 5 minutes | Cook 40 minutes | Serves 4

1 tablespoon olive oil

1 onion, finely diced

1 garlic clove, crushed or grated

500 g (1 lb 2 oz) minced (ground) beef

1 teaspoon ground coriander

1 teaspoon ground cumin

¼ teaspoon salt

100 g (3½ oz) tomato paste (concentrated purée)

12 tacos

1 avocado, diced

½ iceberg lettuce, finely sliced

2 tomatoes, diced

125 g (4½ oz/1 cup) grated cheddar

250 g (9 oz/1 cup) sour cream

Salsa

1 × 400 g (14 oz) tin diced tomatoes

1 teaspoon pickled jalapeño chilli liquid

½ green capsicum (bell pepper), finely diced

pinch of salt

1. Heat the oil in a medium saucepan. Add the onion and garlic and fry until translucent.

2. Add the meat and stir until brown, breaking it up as you go, then add the coriander, cumin, salt, tomato paste and 125 ml (4 fl oz/½ cup) water. Bring to the boil, then reduce the heat and simmer for at least 30 minutes. The meat mix should be quite dry. Adjust the seasoning if required. *If doubling up the recipe, split the mixture in two and allow the extra meal to cool to room temperature. Refrigerate overnight before freezing for later use.*

3. While the meat cooks, make the salsa. Combine all the ingredients in a small saucepan, bring to the boil, then reduce the heat and simmer for 20 minutes. Set aside to cool.

4. In the meantime, preheat the oven and heat the tacos according to the packet instructions.

5. Place all other ingredients in bowls in the centre of the table.

6. When the tacos are heated through, serve immediately.

7. Freeze any leftover tomato salsa for next time in a zip-lock bag or freezer-proof container.

 You can fast-track by using a store-bought chunky salsa if you are short on time.

Italian Meatballs

The key to these great Italian meatballs is the combination of the veal and pork mince, or pork and turkey mince. The mustard gives them a little zing, too. The meatballs without the sauce are perfect for lunch boxes.

Prep 10 minutes | Cook 45 minutes | Serves 4

2 tablespoons olive oil

1 onion, finely diced

1 garlic clove, crushed or grated

500 g (1 lb 2 oz) minced (ground) veal and pork (or use pork and beef or turkey)

50 g (1¾ oz/½ cup) breadcrumbs

1 tablespoon dijon mustard

4 flat-leaf (Italian) parsley sprigs, leaves picked, finely chopped

1 egg

½ teaspoon salt

75 g (2¾ oz/½ cup) plain (all-purpose) flour

2 × 400 g (14 oz) tins diced tomatoes

pasta of your choice, to serve

grated parmesan, to serve

1. Heat 1 tablespoon of the oil in a large frying pan and cook the onion and garlic on a low heat for around 5 minutes. Do not brown the onion. Remove the onion mixture from the pan and set aside to cool.

2. Place the meat, breadcrumbs, mustard, parsley, egg, salt, some pepper and the cooled onion in a large bowl and mix.

3. Use your hands to roll the mixture into 3 cm (1¼ in) meatballs.

4. Place the flour on a plate or in a baking dish and roll the meatballs in the flour to coat. Dust off any excess.

5. Heat the remaining olive oil in a clean frying pan and brown the meatballs. You may need to work in batches to avoid overcrowding the pan.

6. Return all the meatballs to the pan, then carefully add the tinned tomatoes and 200 ml (7 fl oz) water (be cautious: the pan will be hot and might spit). Cover and simmer for 25 minutes. *If doubling up the recipe, split the mixture in two and allow the extra meal to cool to room temperature. Refrigerate overnight before freezing for later use.*

7. While the meatballs are cooking, cook the pasta in a large saucepan of salted water according to the packet instructions.

8. Strain the pasta, top with the meatballs and sauce and sprinkle with parmesan.

 Meatballs are great in a sandwich or a roll the next day, if you have leftovers.

Grecian Beef

The beauty of this Grecian beef dish is that both the meat lovers and the vegetable lovers in your house will be happy. The meat adds a lovely flavour to the vegetables, and I often leave the beef for the rest of the family and just enjoy the vegetables in this great one-pot recipe.

Prep 20 minutes | Cook 2½ hours | Serves 4

2 tablespoons olive oil

600 g (1 lb 5 oz) chuck steak

1 onion, finely diced

2 garlic cloves, crushed or grated

2 carrots, finely diced

1 celery stalk, finely diced

1 zucchini (courgette), finely diced

1 eggplant (aubergine), diced

1 red capsicum (bell pepper), diced

1 teaspoon paprika

4 flat-leaf (Italian) parsley sprigs, leaves picked, chopped

1 bay leaf

1 × 400 g (14 oz) tin diced tomatoes

1 teaspoon salt

100 g (3½ oz/½ cup) jasmine rice

crusty bread, to serve

1. Preheat the oven to 160°C (320°F/Gas Mark 3).

2. Place a wide-based ovenproof pot on the stove. Heat half the olive oil over a medium heat.

3. Sear the beef on both sides, then remove from the pot and set aside.

4. Add the remaining olive oil to the pot and fry the onion, garlic, carrot and celery. Moisten with a little water and cook for 5 minutes over a low heat.

5. Add the zucchini, eggplant and capsicum. Turn up the heat and cook until the eggplant is brown.

6. Add the paprika, parsley, bay leaf and tomatoes with 500 ml (17 fl oz/2 cups) water, plus the salt and some pepper. Bring to the boil, then return the meat to the pot. The liquid should cover the meat and vegetables. Top up with more water if required.

7. Place a piece of baking paper on the surface of the mixture, then cover the pot with a lid. Cook in the oven for 1½–2 hours. If your pot cannot be transferred to the oven, you can simmer the beef on the stove over a very low heat for 1½–2 hours instead. Turn the meat halfway through cooking.

8. Check the meat is cooked by pulling a piece apart with tongs. It should fall apart easily. *If doubling up the recipe, split the mixture in two and allow the extra meal to cool to room temperature. Refrigerate overnight before freezing for later use.*

9. Once the meat is cooked, add the rice, give the dish a stir and return to the oven for 15–20 minutes. Check the rice is cooked before removing from the oven.

10. Pull the meat apart with tongs and stir to combine, then serve with bread.

 The meat should just break into pieces when it is being served. If it doesn't, you may need to continue cooking it for another 20 minutes.

Italian Sausage & White Bean Braise

Italian sausage and white bean braise is a super-easy start-up variation on meatballs. The key is to buy good-quality pork and fennel sausages, either at your local butcher or the supermarket.

Prep 10 minutes | Cook 45 minutes | Serves 4

1 tablespoon olive oil

1 onion, finely diced

1 garlic clove, crushed or grated

1 carrot, finely diced

1 celery stalk, finely diced

4 flat-leaf (Italian) parsley sprigs, leaves picked, chopped

300 g (10½ oz) Italian sausages (such as pork and fennel)

125 ml (4 fl oz/½ cup) red wine (optional)

1 × 400 g (14 oz) tin diced tomatoes

2 × 400 g (14 oz) tins cannellini (lima) beans, drained and rinsed

crusty bread, to serve

1. Heat the oil in a saucepan and cook the onion, garlic, carrot, celery and parsley for 10 minutes. Add a little water to stop it from sticking.

2. Squeeze the sausage mix out of the skins into small balls directly into the pot. Colour the meat on all sides.

3. Add the red wine (if using), tomatoes, beans and 250 ml (8½ fl oz/1 cup) water.

4. Bring to the boil, then reduce the heat, cover with a lid and simmer for 30 minutes.

5. Adjust the seasoning by adding salt and pepper to taste, and serve with bread. *If doubling up the recipe, split the mixture in two and allow the extra meal to cool to room temperature. Refrigerate overnight before freezing for later use.*

 Use butter or borlotti (cranberry) beans if you don't have cannellini beans.

Lamb Kibbeh

These lamb kibbeh are a much cheaper alternative to visiting your local kebab shop. Use store-bought tabbouleh, make your own (see page 201) or simply replace with tomato and lettuce.

Prep 5 minutes | Cook 40 minutes | Serves 4

90 g (3 oz/½ cup) burghul (bulgur wheat)

1 onion, peeled

1 garlic clove, peeled

2 teaspoons ground cinnamon

2 teaspoons ground allspice

1 teaspoon ground sumac

600 g (1 lb 5 oz) minced (ground) lamb

1 teaspoon salt

2 tablespoons olive oil

Lebanese or Turkish bread

400 g (14 oz/2 cups) Tabbouleh (page 201), or use store-bought tabbouleh

125 g (4½ oz/½ cup) plain or Greek yoghurt

tomato sauce (ketchup)

Sriracha sauce (optional)

1. Soak the burghul for 20 minutes, drain and squeeze out any excess water.

2. While the burghul is soaking, blend the onion and garlic to a purée in a food processor.

3. Add the cinnamon, allspice, sumac, lamb, salt and some pepper, and blend to combine. The mixture should resemble a sticky paste.

4. Transfer the lamb mix to a bowl and add the burghul. Using your hands, mix until well combined.

5. Using a spoon or wet hands, roll the mixture into dessert spoon-sized oval shapes and place on a plate. *If doubling the recipe, freeze one meal at this point.*

6. Cook the kibbeh on a barbecue chargrill plate or in a non-stick frying pan with the oil over a medium heat, turning regularly until brown and cooked through, about 6–8 minutes.

7. Serve with bread, tabbouleh, yoghurt and sauces.

 This mix can be made and shaped, then frozen for another time.

Shepherd's Pie

We love a comfort meal such as shepherd's pie when the weather turns a little cooler. Using sweet potato makes this a lower-carb alternative to the traditional white potato shepherd's pie, but either kind is fine to use. A great family favourite that pleases the young and young at heart.

Prep 5 minutes | Cook 1 hour | Serves 4

1 kg (2 lb 3 oz) sweet potato

3 tablespoons olive oil

1 onion, finely diced

2 carrots, diced

1 celery stalk, diced

600 g (1 lb 5 oz) minced (ground) lamb

2 tablespoons tomato paste (concentrated purée)

1 tablespoon worcestershire sauce

1 bay leaf

130 g (4½ oz/1 cup) frozen peas

 This is a great meal to assemble the day before and then heat through in the oven at 180°C (350°F/Gas Mark 4) when ready to serve. You can also freeze it already assembled, or double the meat mixture and freeze for later and simply cook the sweet potato on the day.

1. Preheat oven to 160°C (320°F/Gas Mark 3).

2. Wash the sweet potatoes and cut in half lengthways.

3. Line a baking tray with baking paper and sprinkle the paper with 1 tablespoon of the oil and some salt. Place the sweet potatoes, cut side down, on the tray. Transfer to the oven and cook for 40 minutes, or until soft.

4. While the potatoes are cooking, heat 1 tablespoon oil in a large saucepan. Add the onion, carrot and celery and cook for 10 minutes, taking care not to colour the vegetables. Add a little water if they are sticking to the pan.

5. Add the meat and brown, breaking up any clumps as you go. Add the tomato paste, worcestershire sauce, bay leaf, 250 ml (8½ fl oz/1 cup) water and some salt and pepper. Bring to the boil, then reduce the heat and simmer for 40 minutes. Add the peas in the last 5 minutes of cooking. *If doubling up the recipe, split the mixture in two and allow the extra meal to cool to room temperature. Refrigerate overnight before freezing for later use.*

6. When the potatoes are cooked, remove from the oven and scoop the flesh out of the skin with a spoon. Place in a bowl and mash with a fork.

7. Assemble the pie, either as individual serves in ramekins, or in a larger baking dish as a single pie. Place the meat mixture at the bottom (preheat first if using Foodbanked meat mix), and then top with the mash. Sprinkle with the remaining olive oil.

8. Heat the grill to 180°C (350°F/Gas Mark 4), then place the pie under the grill for about 5 minutes to dry out the sweet potato. Watch it carefully to make sure it doesn't burn.

9. Serve immediately.

Plan Buy Cook

Lamb Tagine

The preserved lemon in this dish imparts a beautiful flavour. Make your own or pick them up at farmers' markets. Use one-quarter of a preserved lemon for this dish, but remember to wash the salt off, discard the flesh and just use the skin.

Prep 15 minutes | Cook 2 hours | Serves 4

1 tablespoon olive oil

1 onion, finely diced

1 garlic clove, crushed or grated

1 carrot, finely diced

1 celery stalk, finely diced

¼ teaspoon ground turmeric

¼ teaspoon ground ginger

2 teaspoons ground coriander

2 teaspoons ground cumin

750 g (1 lb 11 oz) lamb shoulder, diced

2 × 400 g (14 oz) tins diced tomatoes

1 bay leaf

1 cinnamon stick

2 thyme sprigs

1 teaspoon salt

¼ preserved lemon or juice and zest of 1 lemon

85 g (3 oz/½ cup) green olives, halved

1 quantity Failsafe Couscous (page 206), to serve

125 g (4½ oz/½ cup) plain or Greek yoghurt

fresh coriander (cilantro), to garnish

1. Heat the oil in a large saucepan and cook the onion, garlic, carrot and celery over a low heat for about 15 minutes until soft but not brown. Add a little water if it begins to stick.

2. Increase the heat, add the spices and cook for 3 minutes.

3. Add the lamb, turning to brown on all sides. Add the tinned tomatoes, bay leaf, cinnamon, thyme, salt, some pepper and enough water to cover the meat.

4. Bring to the boil, then simmer gently with the lid on for 1½ hours, or place a piece of baking paper on the surface of the meat, cover the pan with a lid and cook in the oven at 160°C (320°F/Gas Mark 3) for 1½ hours.

5. Remove the pith from the preserved lemon, if using. Rinse and finely chop.

6. Remove the lamb tagine from the stove or oven, then add the olives, preserved lemon (or lemon juice and zest) and check the seasoning. Return to the stove or oven for a further 15 minutes. *If doubling up the recipe, split the mixture in two and allow the extra meal to cool to room temperature. Refrigerate overnight before freezing for later use.*

7. In the meantime, cook the couscous according to the recipe on page 206.

8. Serve with couscous, yoghurt and coriander.

 Gather all the spices and measure them into a bowl at the start to save time.

Middle Eastern Meatballs

For an alternative to traditional Italian meatballs, try these tasty Middle Eastern meatballs, which use lamb as a base. They are delicious with Lebanese bread, yoghurt and a simple side salad.

Prep 5 minutes | Cook 1 hour | Serves 4

3 tablespoons olive oil

100 g (3½ oz) tomato paste (concentrated purée)

1 × 400 g (14 oz) tin diced tomatoes

pinch of caster (superfine) sugar

1 onion, finely diced

600 g (1 lb 5 oz) minced (ground) lamb

½ teaspoon ground allspice

½ teaspoon ground cinnamon

pinch of ground turmeric

½ teaspoon salt

plain or Greek yoghurt, to serve

Lebanese bread, to serve

1. To make the sauce, heat 1 tablespoon of the oil in a large saucepan and fry the tomato paste for 1–2 minutes. Don't let it burn.

2. Add the tomatoes, 500 ml (17 fl oz/2 cups) water, the sugar and some salt and pepper. Bring to the boil, then reduce the heat and simmer while you make the meatballs.

3. In a sauté pan or large frying pan, heat another tablespoon of the oil and fry the onion until translucent. You may need to add a little water if it is sticking. Remove from the heat and allow to cool.

4. In a bowl, combine the lamb, spices and salt, and the cooled onions. Form into 5 cm (2 in) balls and set aside.

5. Put the frying pan back over a high heat and add the remaining oil. Brown the meatballs in batches, then place them in the tomato sauce and simmer for 30 minutes until completely cooked. *If doubling up the recipe, split the mixture in two and allow the extra meal to cool to room temperature. Refrigerate overnight before freezing for later use.*

6. Drizzle with yoghurt, then serve with bread.

 Store any leftover sauce and use it for baked eggs. Bring the sauce to the boil, crack a few eggs into it, then spoon the sauce over the eggs and simmer for about 5 minutes. Sprinkle with feta and serve.

Lamb Curry

As much as I love Indian takeaway, curries from shops are rich in ghee. This curry has a lot of flavour without too much fat – the perfect combination.

Prep 15 minutes | Cook 2 hours | Serves 4

1 cinnamon stick

1 bay leaf

4 black peppercorns

4 cardamom pods, lightly bruised

4 whole cloves

2 onions, peeled

3 garlic cloves, peeled

2 teaspoons grated fresh ginger

1 teaspoon ground turmeric

1 tablespoon ground coriander

2 teaspoons ground cumin

2 tablespoons olive oil

750 g (1 lb 11 oz) lamb shoulder, diced

1 tomato, diced

1 teaspoon salt

125 g (4½ oz/½ cup) plain or Greek yoghurt

1 quantity Perfect Steamed Rice (page 205), to serve

1 teaspoon garam masala

100 g (3½ oz/2 cups) baby spinach or 250 g (9 oz) frozen spinach

1. To make the spice mixture, combine the cinnamon stick, bay leaf, peppercorns, cardamom pods and cloves in a bowl and set aside.

2. Blend the onions, garlic, ginger, turmeric, coriander and cumin in a food processor and set aside.

3. Heat the oil in a large saucepan and fry the spice mixture until fragrant.

4. Add the diced lamb and turn to brown on all sides, then remove the lamb and spices from the pan and set aside.

5. Heat the remaining oil in the saucepan, add the puréed onion mix and cook for 10 minutes, stirring continuously. You may need to add a little water to stop it from sticking.

6. Return the meat and spices to the pot, add the tomato, salt, half the yoghurt and enough water to come just below the top of the meat.

7. Bring to the boil, then place a piece of baking paper on the surface of the meat, cover the pan with a lid and simmer over a very low heat for 1½ hours. Alternatively, transfer to the oven preheated to 160°C (320°F/Gas Mark 3) and cook, covered, for 1½ hours, or until the meat is tender.

8. About 15 minutes before the lamb is finished, steam the rice (see page 205, or according to the packet instructions).

9. When the meat is tender, remove the whole spices. Add the garam masala and spinach just prior to serving. *If doubling up the recipe, split the mixture in two and allow the extra meal to cool to room temperature. Refrigerate overnight before freezing for later use.*

10. Serve with steamed rice and the remaining yoghurt.

 To make yellow rice, add a pinch of ground turmeric to the rice and water before cooking.

Lamb Fricassée

A fricassée is traditionally thickened with an egg yolk and cream. I have done away with this and made a simpler version using cornflour. Some sautéed mushrooms make a great addition to this dish.

Prep 10 minutes | Cook 1 hour 40 minutes | Serves 4

600 g (1 lb 5 oz) lamb shoulder, diced and fat removed

1 tablespoon olive oil

1 onion, finely diced

8 flat-leaf (Italian) parsley sprigs, leaves picked, chopped

250 ml (8½ fl oz/1 cup) chicken stock

¼ teaspoon salt

1 tablespoon cornflour (cornstarch)

4 floury potatoes, mashed

steamed vegetables of your choice, to serve

1. Place the lamb in a large saucepan and cover with cold water. Bring to the boil, skim off any impurities that rise to the surface, then strain. Set the lamb aside.

2. Clean the saucepan, then heat the oil over a medium heat. Cook the onion for 5 minutes until translucent.

3. Add the parsley, then return the meat to the pan along with the stock, salt and some pepper.

4. Bring to the boil, then place a piece of baking paper on the surface of the meat and cover the pan with a lid. Simmer for 1½ hours.

5. After 1½ hours, check the lamb is tender. Mix the cornflour with 2 tablespoons water. Bring the lamb back to the boil and stir in the cornflour mixture to thicken. *If doubling up the recipe, split the mixture in two and allow the extra meal to cool to room temperature. Refrigerate overnight before freezing for later use.*

6. Check the seasoning, then serve with mashed potato and steamed vegetables.

The best cut of lamb for this recipe is shoulder. It is not as dry as leg meat and is good for slow cooking.

Vegetable Lasagne

Vegetable lasagne is a lovely alternative to bolognese-based lasagne. Cook the eggplant, zucchini and pumpkin the day before to speed up the process on the evening you are eating it, as it doesn't take long to assemble.

Prep 15 minutes | Cook 2 hours | Serves 4

1 eggplant (aubergine), cut lengthways into 1 cm (½ in) slices

1 teaspoon salt

400 g (14 oz) pumpkin (winter squash), peeled and cut into 1 cm (½ in) slices

1 shallot, sliced

1 garlic clove, crushed or grated

125 ml (4 fl oz/½ cup) olive oil

1 zucchini (courgette), cut lengthways into 1 cm (½ in slices)

500 ml (17 fl oz/2 cups) chunky tomato passata (puréed tomatoes)

180 g (6½ oz) dried lasagne sheets

250 g (9 oz/1 cup) firm ricotta, crumbled

6 fresh basil sprigs, leaves picked, plus extra, to garnish (optional)

60 g (2 oz) baby spinach leaves

50 g (1¾ oz/½ cup) grated parmesan

green salad, to serve

1. Sprinkle the eggplant slices with salt and set aside in a colander for 30 minutes.

2. Preheat the oven to 180°C (350°F/Gas Mark 4).

3. Place the pumpkin slices on a tray lined with baking paper. Put the sliced shallot and garlic on top and season. Drizzle with 2 tablespoons of the oil, then toss together and spread out on the tray.

4. Place the zucchini slices on a separate baking tray and sprinkle with salt, pepper and 1 tablespoon of the oil. Cook in the oven for 15–20 minutes, or until the vegetables are just soft. After salting, rinse the eggplant and pat dry with paper towel. Spread on a lined baking tray, drizzle with the remaining oil and cook for 20 minutes until soft.

5. Reduce the oven temperature to 160°C (320°F/ Gas Mark 3).

6. Assemble the lasagne in a 30 × 20 cm (12 × 8 in) baking dish. Pour in one-quarter of the passata, then top with a layer of lasagne sheets. Top with another one-quarter of the passata, then add the pumpkin, 200 g (7 oz) of the ricotta and half the basil leaves. Add another layer of lasagne sheets on top, then another one-quarter of the passata, the eggplant, zucchini and baby spinach. Sprinkle with black pepper.

7. Finally, top with another layer of lasagne sheets, the remaining ricotta and basil, and the last of the passata mixed with 125 ml (4 fl oz/½ cup) water. *If doubling up the recipe, assemble the meals in two baking dishes and freeze the extra lasagne (uncooked) for later use.*

8. Cover with baking paper and foil and bake for 30 minutes. Remove and sprinkle with the parmesan. Bake for a further 10 minutes, uncovered.

9. Remove from the oven and leave to stand for 10 minutes before serving. Serve with a green salad and garnish with basil, if desired.

Split Pea Dahl

Dahl in winter is like a big woollen jumper: warm and cosy. This is a great way to get at least three serves of veg in the one meal.

Prep 15 minutes + soaking overnight | Cook 1 hour | Serves 4

200 g (7 oz) green split peas, soaked overnight

1 tablespoon olive oil

1 onion, finely diced

1 garlic clove, crushed or grated

1 teaspoon grated fresh ginger

½ teaspoon cumin seeds

1 tablespoon mild curry powder

200 g (7 oz) sweet potato, peeled and diced

1 quantity Perfect Steamed Rice (page 205), to serve

100 g (3½ oz/2 cups) baby spinach leaves

50 g (1¾ oz) green beans

½ teaspoon salt

1 teaspoon garam masala

pinch of dried chilli flakes

125 g (4½ oz/½ cup) plain or Greek yoghurt

1. Drain the split pea soaking water and rinse them.

2. Heat the oil in a large saucepan over a medium heat and cook the onion, garlic and ginger for 10 minutes until soft.

3. Add the cumin and curry powder and cook for 2 minutes.

4. Next, add the split peas and 750 ml (25½ fl oz/ 3 cups) water, bring to the boil, then lower the heat and simmer, covered, for 25 minutes.

5. Add the sweet potato, cover and simmer for a further 20 minutes, or until soft. You may need to add a little more water at this stage if the mixture seems a bit dry, or the split peas seem too hard.

6. In the meantime, steam the rice according to the recipe on page 205, or follow the packet instructions.

7. Once the sweet potato is soft, add the spinach, green beans, salt and garam masala and cook for 5 minutes.

8. Adjust the seasoning if required. *If doubling up the recipe, split the mixture in two and allow the extra meal to cool to room temperature. Refrigerate overnight before freezing for later use.*

9. Serve with dried chilli flakes, yoghurt and rice.

There are some great varieties of flatbreads in the supermarket. Grill them on the barbecue or in a hot chargrill pan as an alternative to rice, or pick up fresh bread from your local Indian takeaway on your way home.

Bean & Barley Braise

This bean and barley braise is a great, filling vegetarian meal, and makes a nice change from a meat braise. Perfect served with some bread, yoghurt and chilli. The pearl barley really bulks out the dish. Dinner done!

Prep 10 minutes | Cook 1¼ hours | Serves 6–8

1 tablespoon olive oil

1 onion, finely diced

1 garlic clove, crushed or grated

1 celery stalk, finely diced

2 carrots, diced

2 flat-leaf (Italian) parsley sprigs, leaves picked, chopped

1 bay leaf

½ teaspoon ground cinnamon

1 teaspoon ground cumin

1 teaspoon ground coriander

1 × 400 g (14 oz) tin brown lentils, drained and rinsed

1 × 400 g (14 oz) tin borlotti (cranberry) beans, drained and rinsed

1 × 400 g (14 oz) tin cannellini (lima) beans, drained and rinsed

1 × 400 g (14 oz) tin chickpeas, drained and rinsed

2 × 400 g (14 oz) tins diced tomatoes

500 ml (17 fl oz/2 cups) vegetable stock

55 g (2 oz/¼ cup) pearl barley

plain or Greek yoghurt, dried chilli flakes and bread, to serve

1. Heat the oil in a large saucepan and cook the onion, garlic, celery and carrot for about 10 minutes over a low heat.

2. Add the parsley, bay leaf and spices and stir until fragrant, about 2 minutes.

3. Add the lentils, beans, chickpeas, tomatoes and 250 ml (8½ fl oz/1 cup) water.

4. Bring to the boil, then reduce the heat and simmer for 40 minutes.

5. Meanwhile, bring the stock to the boil in a separate saucepan, then add the barley and cook for 20 minutes.

6. Drain the barley, add it to the bean mix and cook for another 5 minutes. *If doubling up the recipe, split the mixture in two and allow the extra meal to cool to room temperature. Refrigerate overnight before freezing for later use.*

7. Serve with yoghurt, dried chilli and bread.

If you are gluten-free, substitute the pearl barley with brown rice.

Napolitana Pasta Sauce

For pizza, pasta or vegetarian lasagne – look no further than this versatile recipe. Napolitana or Napoletana? However you spell it, this sauce tastes great.

Prep 5 minutes | Cook 2 hours | Serves 4

3 tablespoons olive oil

4 garlic cloves, peeled

2 celery stalks, halved

1 carrot, halved lengthways

1 onion, peeled and halved

2 × 400 g (14 oz) tins diced tomatoes

2 fresh basil sprigs

2 teaspoons balsamic vinegar

1 teaspoon salt

1 teaspoon caster (superfine) sugar

pasta of your choice, to serve

grated parmesan, to serve

1. Heat the olive oil in a large saucepan and add the garlic, celery, carrot and onion. Cook over a low heat for about 10 minutes, then add the tomatoes, 250 ml (8½ fl oz/1 cup) water, the basil, vinegar, salt and sugar.

2. Bring to the boil, then reduce the heat and simmer for 1–2 hours.

3. Just before the end of the cooking time, cook the pasta according to the packet instructions.

4. Remove the onion, garlic, carrot, celery and basil stalks. *If doubling up the recipe, split the mixture in two and allow the extra meal to cool to room temperature. Refrigerate overnight before freezing for later use.*

5. Spoon the sauce over the pasta, sprinkle with parmesan and serve.

Leftover parmesan rinds are great in this sauce – add them with the tomatoes and remove with the vegetables at the end.

Chicken & Corn Soup

We just cannot get enough soup in the colder months, and this chicken and corn version ticks all the right boxes. A simple combination of ginger, corn and spring onions with poached chicken, it freezes beautifully for additional serves in later weeks or for lunches.

Prep 10 minutes | Cook 50 minutes | Serves 4

2 corn cobs, husks removed

200 g (7 oz) chicken breast

8 spring onions (scallions), roots removed, 4 left whole, 4 sliced

1 × 4 cm (1½ in) piece fresh ginger, half sliced, half grated

1 litre (34 fl oz/4 cups) chicken stock

1 tablespoon olive oil

1 garlic clove, crushed or grated

2 teaspoons light soy sauce

¼ teaspoon salt

pinch of ground white pepper

 You can always use tinned or frozen corn if you are time poor.

1. Place the corn cobs in a saucepan of cold water with a pinch of salt. Bring to the boil and simmer for 20 minutes.

2. Drain the corn cobs. Once cool enough to handle, remove the corn from the cobs using a sharp knife.

3. In a saucepan, combine the chicken breast, whole spring onions, sliced ginger and chicken stock. Bring to the boil, then cover, reduce the heat and simmer for 10 minutes. Remove from the heat, leaving the chicken breast in the liquid.

4. Heat the oil in a saucepan and cook the sliced spring onion (reserving some to garnish) for 3 minutes over a medium heat, then add the garlic and grated ginger.

5. Cook for a further 3 minutes, adding a few tablespoons of the chicken poaching liquid to help cook the ginger and garlic without burning.

6. Remove the chicken breast and set aside. Strain the poaching liquid into the spring onion, ginger and garlic mix, then add the soy sauce, salt and corn. Bring to the boil and simmer for 20 minutes.

7. While the soup is simmering, shred the chicken breast and set aside.

8. Once the soup is cooked, take half the soup out of the pot and blend using a hand-held blender or food processor.

9. Return the blended soup to the pot. Add the shredded chicken and white pepper, and adjust the seasoning if required. *If doubling up the recipe, split the mixture in two and allow the extra meal to cool to room temperature. Refrigerate overnight before freezing for later use.*

10. Serve with the remaining spring onions on top.

See image on page 118.

Plan Buy Cook

Minestrone

Warm up with minestrone. A hearty minestrone is a meal in itself. It is the perfect use for any vegetables leftover in your crisper. Pre-cook the pasta so that it doesn't soak up all the liquid from the soup.

Prep 15 minutes | Cook 2½ hours | Serves 4

200 g (7 oz) smoked bacon bones

2 tablespoons olive oil

1 onion, finely diced

1 celery stalk, finely diced

2 carrots, finely diced

1 zucchini (courgette), finely diced

1 potato, peeled and cut into chunks

1 garlic clove, crushed or grated

4 flat-leaf (Italian) parsley sprigs, leaves picked, chopped

1 × 400 g (14 oz) tin diced tomatoes

1 parmesan rind (from a parmesan block)

1 bay leaf

50 g (1¾ oz/⅓ cup) macaroni

1 × 400 g (14 oz) tin cannellini (lima) beans, drained and rinsed

50 g (1¾ oz/½ cup) grated parmesan

1. Place the bacon bones in a large saucepan with 1 litre (34 fl oz/4 cups) water. Bring to the boil, then reduce the heat and simmer for 1 hour to make a stock.

2. Heat the oil in another large stockpot or saucepan, add the onion and cook over a low heat for 10 minutes.

3. Add the celery, carrot, zucchini, potato, garlic and parsley, and continue to cook for 20 minutes, stirring frequently.

4. Add the stock from step 1, the tomatoes, parmesan rind and bay leaf. Bring to the boil, then simmer for 1½ hours. *If doubling up the recipe, split the mixture in two and allow the extra meal to cool to room temperature. Refrigerate overnight before freezing for later use.*

5. Meanwhile, cook the macaroni according to the packet instructions and set aside.

6. After 1½ hours, add the cannellini beans and the macaroni to the soup.

7. Cook for another 5 minutes, then serve sprinkled with parmesan cheese.

See image on page 119, top.

Cabbage and spinach can easily find a home in this dish, along with any winter root vegetables. Make the stock earlier in the week to cut down cooking time.

Arun's Lentil Soup

I worked with Arun a few years ago, and he would put this dish on the menu in the winter months. With only eight main ingredients and very little prep, Arun's lentil soup can be on the table in an hour once you have soaked the lentils. Perfect for either a mid-winter lunch or dinner. And as a bonus, it is also vegan.

Prep 5 minutes + 1 hour soaking time |
Cook 1 hour | Serves 4

250 g (9 oz/1 cup) red lentils, soaked for 1 hour

1 tablespoon olive oil

1 onion, finely diced

1 garlic clove, crushed or grated

1 teaspoon cumin seeds

2 tomatoes, chopped

20 fresh curry leaves

dried chilli flakes

1. Drain and rinse the lentils and set aside.

2. Heat the oil in a large saucepan and cook the onion and garlic for 10 minutes without colouring them. Add a splash of water if they begin to stick.

3. Toss in the cumin seeds and cook, stirring continuously, until they become fragrant.

4. Add the tomatoes, curry leaves and lentils, stir, then add 1 litre (34 fl oz/4 cups) water. Bring to the boil and simmer for 45 minutes.

5. *If doubling up the recipe, split the mixture in two and allow the extra meal to cool to room temperature. Refrigerate overnight before freezing for later use.*

6. Check for seasoning, ladle into bowls and serve with chilli flakes on top.

   See image on page 119, centre.

 The curry leaves are edible. It is a personal choice whether you eat them or leave them on the side of the bowl. You can freeze any remaining curry leaves and use them next time you make this soup, or in a curry.

Plan Buy Cook

Mulligatawny Soup

Mulligatawny was made famous by Seinfeld's Soup Nazi. The recipe is delicious and filling, and a great mid-season meal.

Prep 25 minutes | Cook 1 hour 5 minutes | Serves 4

1 tablespoon olive oil

1 onion, chopped

1 garlic clove, crushed or grated

1 carrot, diced

1 celery stalk, diced

1 teaspoon grated fresh ginger

2 tablespoons tomato paste (concentrated purée)

1 tomato, chopped

1 tablespoon mild curry powder

1 green apple, grated

1 potato, peeled and diced

1 chicken breast

1 teaspoon salt

50 g (1¾ oz/¼ cup) jasmine rice

1. Heat the oil in a large saucepan and cook the onion, garlic, carrot, celery and ginger for 15 minutes, adding a bit of water to stop it from browning.

2. Add the tomato paste, tomato and curry powder, and cook for a few more minutes.

3. Add 1 litre (34 fl oz/4 cups) water, the apple, potato, chicken, salt and some pepper. Bring to the boil, then reduce the heat and simmer for 30 minutes.

4. Remove the chicken breast, shred the meat and return it to the pot. *If doubling up the recipe, split the mixture in two and allow the extra meal to cool to room temperature. Refrigerate overnight before freezing for later use.*

5. Add the rice and simmer for a further 10–15 minutes.

6. Adjust the consistency by mashing some of the potatoes with the back of a fork if you prefer a thicker soup, or add a little water if the soup is too thick.

7. Adjust the seasoning and serve.

   See image on page 119, bottom.

I love the green apple – it adds both tartness and sweetness to this soup.

Lemongrass Beef Marinade

This marinade is great served with greens, steamed rice and quick-pickle vegetables.

Prep 5 minutes + marinating time of 1+ hour | Cook 20 minutes | Serves 4

1 lemongrass stem, white part only, chopped or finely grated

1 garlic clove, peeled

1 shallot, peeled

2 tablespoons light soy sauce

2 tablespoons brown sugar

¼ teaspoon chilli flakes

600 g (1 lb 5 oz) rump steak

1 quantity Perfect Steamed Rice (page 205), to serve

Steamed Asian Greens (page 205)

1. Make the marinade for the beef by combining the lemongrass, garlic, shallot, soy sauce, brown sugar and chilli in a food processor. Blend to a paste, then set aside.

2. Slice the beef against the grain into long strips, then toss in the marinade. Leave to marinate for at least 1 hour. *If doubling the recipe, freeze the extra meal in its marinade, uncooked, for later use.*

3. Steam the rice according to the recipe on page 205, or follow the packet instructions.

4. Heat a barbecue chargrill plate or chargrill pan over a high heat and cook the beef, turning once. It will only take 2–3 minutes per side.

5. Serve with steamed rice and Asian greens.

 You could use sliced chicken instead of beef if you prefer. Also great in banh mi with quick pickled vegetables.

Indian Chicken Marinade

We love this simple Indian chicken marinade either in a wrap or served with a simple salad or rice. It is made from just four key ingredients that you generally have at home.

Prep 10 minutes + marinating time of 4+ hours | **Cook 30 minutes** | **Serves 4**

350 g (12½ oz) plain or Greek yoghurt

3 teaspoons garam masala

1 teaspoon ground turmeric

1 teaspoon ground coriander

¼ teaspoon salt

600 g (1 lb 5 oz) boneless chicken thighs

olive oil, for greasing

4 naan or roti breads

1 Lebanese (short) cucumber, finely diced

2 tablespoons mango chutney

100 g (3½ oz/2 cups) baby spinach

1. Mix 250 g (9 oz/1 cup) of the yoghurt, the garam masala, turmeric, coriander and salt in a bowl, then add the chicken thighs.

2. Marinate overnight or for at least 4 hours in the fridge. *If doubling the recipe, freeze the extra meal in its marinade, uncooked, for later use.*

3. Heat a barbecue chargrill plate or chargrill pan over a very high heat. Rub the plate or bars with a little oil on some paper towel and cook the meat for 7–8 minutes per side.

4. Transfer to a warm plate, cover with foil and rest for 10 minutes. Cook the bread on the grill.

5. Mix the remaining yoghurt, cucumber and some salt together.

6. Serve with chutney, bread, spinach and the cucumber yoghurt.

See image on page 122.

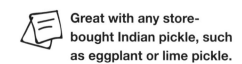

Great with any store-bought Indian pickle, such as eggplant or lime pickle.

Easy Asian Skewers

Kids love food on a stick. This marinade is equally good with either beef or chicken. You can swap the sambal oelek with red curry paste.

Prep 20 minutes + marinating time of 4+ hours | Cook 30 minutes | Serves 4

12 bamboo skewers

600 g (1 lb 5 oz) beef rump or boneless chicken thighs

1 lemongrass stem

2 teaspoons sambal oelek

2 garlic cloves, crushed

pinch of ground turmeric

3 tablespoons light soy sauce

2 tablespoons brown sugar

80 ml (2½ fl oz/⅓ cup) coconut cream

1 quantity Perfect Steamed Rice (page 205), to serve

olive oil, for greasing

satay sauce, to serve (optional)

salad, to serve (optional)

Steamed Asian Greens (page 205), to serve (optional)

1. Soak the bamboo skewers in water for 20 minutes. Dice the beef or chicken into 2 cm (¾ in) pieces.

2. Remove the outer layer from the lemongrass stem. Grate the root end, about 3 cm (1¼ in) up the stalk.

3. Mix the grated lemongrass, sambal oelek, garlic, turmeric, soy sauce, sugar and coconut cream in a bowl. Add the meat to coat and thread onto the skewers. Place the skewers in a baking dish and pour the remaining marinade over the top. Marinate overnight or for at least 4 hours in the fridge. *If doubling the recipe, freeze the extra meal in its marinade, uncooked, for later use.*

4. Steam the rice according to the recipe on page 205, or follow packet instructions.

5. Heat a barbecue chargrill plate or chargrill pan over a high heat. Rub the plate or bars with a little oil on some paper towel. Barbecue the skewers until cooked, about 4–5 minutes per side.

6. Transfer to a warm plate, cover with foil and rest for 10 minutes.

7. Serve with satay sauce (if using), rice and salad, or Asian greens.

See image on page 122.

 Freeze leftover coconut cream, or use it to make a satay sauce with a store-bought satay paste.

Mango Chicken

This super-fast marinade is always a winner on the barbecue. If you don't have any fresh coriander, you can substitute it with ground coriander instead. Cooking for a crowd? You can't beat this mango chicken recipe for ease.

Prep 5 minutes + marinating time of 4+ hours | Cook 20 minutes | Serves 4

600 g (1 lb 5 oz) boneless chicken thighs

200 g (7 oz) mango chutney

6 fresh coriander (cilantro) sprigs, leaves picked, finely chopped

6 flat-leaf (Italian) parsley sprigs, leaves picked, finely chopped

¼ teaspoon ground turmeric

1 teaspoon ground cumin

juice of ½ lemon

olive oil, for greasing

vegetables or salad, to serve

1. Trim the excess fat from the chicken.

2. In a bowl, mix the chutney, herbs and spices.

3. Add the chicken to the bowl and mix thoroughly. Marinate overnight or for at least 4 hours.
   If doubling the recipe, freeze the extra meal in its marinade, uncooked, for later use.

4. Heat a barbecue chargrill plate or chargrill pan over a medium heat. While it is warming up, squeeze the lemon juice over the chicken. Sprinkle with a little salt before cooking.

5. Rub the plate with a little oil on some paper towel, and cook the chicken thighs for at least 5 minutes each side.

6. Transfer to a warm plate, cover with foil and rest for 10 minutes.

7. Serve with your choice of vegetables or salad.

 Great to serve with the Pumpkin & Couscous Salad on page 202. See Barbecue Basics on page 133.

Barbecued Lamb with Couscous

This is a wonderful, simple summer dish. If you have marinated the meat in advance, it can be on the table in 20 minutes.

Prep 10 minutes + marinating time of 4+ hours | Cook 20 minutes | Serves 4

2 garlic cloves, crushed or grated

3 teaspoons ground cumin

3 teaspoons cracked black pepper

1 tablespoon brown sugar

2 tablespoons olive oil, plus extra for greasing

600 g (1 lb 5 oz) lamb rump, sliced

juice of 1 lemon

1 teaspoon salt

1 quantity Failsafe Couscous (page 206)

4 flat-leaf (Italian) parsley sprigs, leaves picked, chopped

1 shallot, finely diced

1 tomato, chopped

100 g (3½ oz) vegetable relish (ajvar), or harissa

250 g (9 oz/1 cup) plain or Greek yoghurt

1. Mix together the garlic, cumin, pepper, sugar and olive oil in a bowl.

2. Add the lamb, coat well, then cover and refrigerate overnight or for at least 4 hours. *If doubling the recipe, freeze the extra meal in its marinade, uncooked, for later use.*

3. Just before cooking the lamb, add the lemon juice and season with the salt.

4. Heat a barbecue chargrill plate or a chargrill pan over a very high heat. Rub the plate or bars with oil on some paper towel. Cook the lamb to your liking.

5. Transfer to a warm plate, cover with foil and rest for 10 minutes.

6. Cook the couscous according to the recipe on page 206, or follow the packet instructions.

7. Once cooked, add the parsley, shallot and tomato to the couscous.

8. Serve the lamb with the couscous, vegetable relish and yoghurt.

 Use store-bought ajvar or harissa. Choose mild or hot depending on your preference.

Five-spice Marinade

This tasty marinade works well with beef, pork or chicken. Serve with steamed Asian greens and rice. An Asian slaw is also a good match in the warmer months.

Prep 5 minutes + marinating time of 4+ hours | Cook 15 minutes | Serves 4

2 tablespoons honey

2 tablespoons light soy sauce

2 tablespoons oyster sauce

2 garlic cloves, crushed or grated

2 teaspoons Chinese five-spice powder

600 g (1 lb 5 oz) trimmed pork, beef rump or skinless chicken thighs or drumsticks (your choice)

1 quantity Perfect Steamed Rice (page 205), to serve

olive oil, for greasing

Steamed Asian Greens (page 205) or Asian Coleslaw (page 199), to serve

1. Mix together the honey, soy sauce, oyster sauce, garlic and five-spice powder in a bowl.

2. Add the meat of your choice, cover and refrigerate for at least 4 hours, or overnight. *If doubling the recipe, freeze the extra meal in its marinade, uncooked, for later use.*

3. Steam the rice according to the recipe on page 205, or follow the packet instructions.

4. Heat a barbecue chargrill plate or chargrill pan over high heat. Rub the plate or bars with a little oil on some paper towel and cook the meat for about 6 minutes per side, or until cooked through or cooked to your liking.

5. Transfer to a warm plate, cover with foil and rest for 10 minutes.

6. Serve with your choice of steamed rice, vegetables or salad.

See image on page 122.

 This dish only requires a few pantry ingredients – skip pre-marinated meats and make your own.

Greek Pork Skewers

Try these Greek-inspired pork skewers with a Greek salad and tzatziki for a change from traditional Greek lamb dishes. It's lighter on the budget, too. Look for the dried oregano on its stem – available at the green grocer or check your supermarket.

Prep 5 minutes + marinating time of 4+ hours | Cook time: 20 minutes | Serves 4

12 bamboo skewers

1 tablespoon olive oil, plus extra for greasing

1 teaspoon grated lemon zest

1 teaspoon dried oregano

¼ teaspoon cracked black pepper

pinch of dried chilli flakes

1 garlic clove, crushed or grated

600 g (1 lb 5 oz) pork neck, fat trimmed

crusty bread, tzatziki and vegetables or salad, to serve

lemon wedges, to serve

1. Soak the bamboo skewers in water for at least 20 minutes.

2. Combine the oil, lemon zest, oregano, pepper, chilli and garlic in a bowl to form a marinade.

3. Dice the pork into 2 cm (¾ in) pieces, then toss it through the marinade, cover with plastic wrap and refrigerate overnight or for at least 4 hours. *If doubling the recipe, freeze the extra meal in its marinade, uncooked, for later use.*

4. When ready to cook, thread the pork onto skewers and sprinkle with salt. Heat a barbecue chargrill plate or chargrill pan over a high heat. Rub the plate or bars with some oil on paper towel, then barbecue the skewers for 10–15 minutes, turning regularly.

5. Transfer to a warm plate, cover with foil and rest for 10 minutes.

6. Serve warm with bread, tzatziki, vegetables or salad and lemon wedges on the side.

See image on page 132.

 Pork neck is often labelled pork scotch.

Make your own tzatziki by combining Greek yoghurt, grated garlic, cumin, grated cucumber, salt and some fresh mint.

BBQ Basics

How much do we love cooking on a barbecue? Taking your cooking outdoors is a great warm-weather option. Here are our tips on how to barbecue like a pro.

PREPARING YOUR BARBECUE

Heat the plate or bars, then put some oil on a rag or paper towel and generously rub the plate or bars with oil. By rubbing the oil onto the barbecue, the meat doesn't stick.

FYI: The meat will tend to stick to the barbecue if the plate is not hot enough.

PREPARING THE MEAT

Take any meat out of the fridge about 1 hour before you plan to cook it. This is especially important when cooking rare to medium–rare steaks. Season the meat with salt before you barbecue.

 When cooking for large groups, sear the meat on both sides to get grill marks, then finish cooking the meat in the oven for 10–15 minutes, or longer for larger quantities. Preheat it to 160°C (320°F/Gas Mark 3).

MASTER SOME MARINADES

Marinated meats tend to burn faster than steak and sausages, so make sure you turn your meat quickly. Once the meat is sealed on all sides, reduce the heat to cook the meat through without burning it. Another option is to transfer the meat to the oven to finish it if you are nervous about burning or undercooking it (see Tip above).

CHARGRILLING VEGETABLES

Use your barbecue to chargrill vegetables such as eggplant (aubergine), corn, capsicum (bell pepper), zucchini (courgette), mushrooms, cauliflower, broccoli and asparagus. Toss the vegetables in oil and salt and leave them for about 10 minutes before you start cooking them. Use the bars to get grill marks on the vegetables for a great look. Sprinkle with balsamic vinegar, olive oil and fresh basil leaves, then serve.

OTHER GREAT THINGS TO BARBECUE

Get more use out of your barbecue by cooking Hamburgers (page 88), bacon, eggs, kibbeh (page 97), falafel (page 143), fish, haloumi cheese, tinned sardines: the list is endless. It is a great way to keep your kitchen clean and take some of the smells outdoors.

CLEANING THE BARBECUE

It doesn't matter whether you clean your barbecue after you've finished cooking or before you use it the next time, but clean it you must. Heat the barbecue and use a good wire brush for the bars and a metal scraper for the plate to scrape off excess food scraps, marinade or residue. Once clean, pour on some water and allow it to evaporate. Turn the barbecue off, then use a rag or paper towel to mop up any remaining residue and rub generously with oil to stop it rusting between uses.

If you have ingredients for a few pantry meals on hand, you won't struggle to produce an extra meal out of nowhere if you need to.

Keep your fridge stocked with some basics such as parmesan cheese and plain or Greek yoghurt to accompany pantry meals.

Pantry Tuna Pasta

This tuna pasta recipe is the perfect meal if you are short on time and ingredients. Most of this meal comes out of your pantry, and it is a lifesaver when you need a meal on the table in half an hour.

Prep 5 minutes | Cook 30 minutes | Serves 4

400 g (14 oz) tinned tuna in oil

½ onion, finely diced

2 garlic cloves, crushed or grated

4 flat-leaf (Italian) parsley sprigs,
    leaves picked, chopped

1 × 400 g (14 oz) tin diced tomatoes

¼ teaspoon salt

400 g (14 oz) angel hair pasta

pinch of dried chilli flakes (optional)

grated parmesan, to serve

1. Drain the oil from the tuna into a saucepan.

2. Add the onion, garlic and parsley and cook over a medium heat until fragrant, about 5 minutes.

3. Add the tuna, tomatoes, 200 ml (7 fl oz) water, the salt and some pepper to the pan. Bring to the boil, then reduce the heat and simmer for 20 minutes. *If doubling up the recipe, split the mixture in two and allow the extra meal to cool to room temperature. Refrigerate overnight before freezing for later use.*

4. Meanwhile, bring a large saucepan of salted water to the boil for the pasta. Cook the pasta according to the packet instructions.

5. Strain the pasta and return it to the large saucepan. Pour over the tuna sauce and stir to combine.

6. Serve immediately with dried chilli flakes, if desired, and sprinkle with parmesan.

 This is a great low-waste meal as you cook with the oil from the tuna. Don't worry if you don't have any parsley – it is also fine without it.

Bean Quesadillas

We love bean quesadillas for a great weeknight meal. The ingredients for the bean mix come from the pantry. These quesadillas are also great in the lunchbox the next day. I make mine without cheese, but feel free to add some before you assemble them.

Prep 15 minutes | Cook 50 minutes | Serves 4

1 tablespoon olive oil

1 onion, chopped

2 garlic cloves, crushed or grated

1 teaspoon ground cumin

1 teaspoon ground coriander

1 × 400 g (14 oz) tin diced tomatoes

2 × 400 g (14 oz) tins red kidney beans, drained and rinsed, or 210 g (7½ oz/ 1 cup) dried kidney beans, soaked and cooked (see Note)

8 tortillas

cheddar cheese, grated (optional)

lime wedges, to serve (optional)

125 g (4½ oz/½ cup) plain or Greek yoghurt, or sour cream

2 slices pickled jalapeño chilli

Salsa

100 g (3½ oz/½ cup) corn kernels (tinned or frozen)

1 shallot, finely diced

1 tomato, chopped

8 fresh coriander (cilantro) sprigs, leaves picked, chopped

1. Heat the oil in a saucepan and cook the onion and garlic over a medium heat for 10 minutes.

2. Add the cumin and coriander, stir and cook for 2 minutes. Add 1 tablespoon water if needed to stop the spices burning.

3. Add the tomatoes, kidney beans and salt and pepper to taste.

4. Bring to the boil, then reduce the heat and simmer for 40 minutes, stirring occasionally. The mix needs to be quite dry. *If doubling up the recipe, split the mixture in two and allow the extra meal to cool to room temperature. Refrigerate overnight before freezing for later use.*

5. Heat a non-stick frying pan over a medium heat. Place a tortilla in the pan and spread a few tablespoons of the bean mixture on top. Add the grated cheese, if using. Place another tortilla on top and press down with a spatula, turn over and cook until golden. Alternatively, use a sandwich press or the oven grill. If cooking under the grill, flip to crisp the other side.

6. To make the salsa, combine the corn, shallot, tomato and coriander, then set aside.

7. To serve, cut the quesadillas into quarters, transfer to a plate and top with salsa, yoghurt and jalapeño chilli. Serve with lime wedges, if desired.

 A tablespoon of the pickling liquid from the jalapeño chillies can be added to the bean mix for extra flavour. This recipe is also great as a nacho mix topped with lettuce, diced tomatoes and sour cream or yoghurt.

COOKING BEANS YOURSELF?
Soak dried beans overnight, then rinse. Place in a saucepan with plenty of cold water. Bring to the boil, reduce the heat and simmer until tender (at least 30 minutes). Note that 105 g (3½ oz/½ cup) dried beans is equal to 400 g (14 oz) cooked tinned beans.

Chickpea Curry

This is one of Gaby's share-house recipes from her student days. I made a few adjustments and added garam masala, which adds a great flavour to the dish.

Prep 5 minutes | Cook 1 hour | Serves 4

1 tablespoon olive oil

1 onion, finely diced

2 teaspoons grated fresh ginger

2 garlic cloves, crushed or grated

¼ teaspoon ground turmeric

2 teaspoons ground cumin

2 teaspoons ground coriander

¼ teaspoon ground chilli

1 × 400 g (14 oz) tin diced tomatoes

3 × 400 g (14 oz) tins chickpeas, drained and rinsed, or 330 g (11½ oz/1½ cups) dried chickpeas, soaked and cooked

1 quantity Perfect Steamed Rice (page 205) or bread, to serve

1 teaspoon garam masala

100 g (3½ oz/2 cups) baby spinach

1. Heat the oil in a large saucepan over a medium heat. Add the onion, ginger and garlic and cook for 5 minutes.

2. Add the spices and fry for 2 minutes. Add 1 tablespoon of water if it starts to stick.

3. Add the tomatoes and 300 ml (10 fl oz) water and bring to the boil.

4. Add the chickpeas and simmer for 40 minutes.

5. Steam the rice according to the recipe on page 205, or follow the packet instructions.

6. When ready to serve, add the garam masala and stir through the spinach. *If doubling up the recipe, split the mixture in two and allow the extra meal to cool to room temperature. Refrigerate overnight before freezing for later use.*

7. Serve with rice or bread.

 Use frozen spinach if you don't have any fresh.

COOKING CHICKPEAS YOURSELF?

Soak dried chickpeas overnight, then rinse. Place in a saucepan with plenty of cold water. Bring to the boil, reduce the heat and simmer until tender (at least 90 minutes). Note that 110 g (4 oz/½ cup) dried chickpeas is equal to 400 g (14 oz) cooked chickpeas.

Plan Buy Cook

Puttanesca Sauce

This is one of our easy pantry meals where all of the ingredients (besides the chilli and parmesan) come from the pantry. Dial the heat up or down with the amount of chilli you use. Substitute the fresh chilli for dried chilli flakes if you don't have any chillies in the fridge or freezer.

Prep 10 minutes | Cook 50 minutes | Serves 4

1 tablespoon olive oil

½ onion, finely diced

2 garlic cloves, crushed or grated

2 × 400 g (14 oz) tins diced tomatoes

4 anchovy fillets, chopped

1 red finger chilli, sliced

1 tablespoon capers, rinsed

4 flat-leaf (Italian) parsley sprigs, leaves picked, chopped

pasta of your choice, to serve

12 pitted kalamata olives

grated parmesan, to serve

1. Heat the oil in a large frying pan or saucepan and cook the onion and garlic until soft but not brown.

2. Add the tomatoes and 125 ml (4 fl oz/½ cup) water, then bring to the boil.

3. Reduce the heat to a simmer and add the anchovies, chilli, capers and parsley. Cook over a low heat for 40 minutes.

4. While the sauce is simmering, cook the pasta according to the packet instructions.

5. Add the olives and some pepper to the sauce when cooked. *If doubling up the recipe, split the mixture in two and allow the extra meal to cool to room temperature. Refrigerate overnight before freezing for later use.*

6. Toss the drained pasta through the sauce. Serve with grated cheese.

 To make this a vegetarian sauce, remove the anchovies. This dish also goes well with a leafy green salad.

Plan Buy Cook

Baked Beans

Homemade baked beans are a great source of fibre and are low GI. As an added bonus, this recipe also gives you at least two serves of veggies for the day. You'll never eat tinned baked beans again after trying these.

Prep 10 minutes | Cook 1 hour | Serves 4

1 tablespoon olive oil

1 onion, finely diced

1 garlic clove, crushed or grated

½ green capsicum (bell pepper), diced

1 teaspoon sweet paprika

1 × 400 g (14 oz) tin cannellini (lima) beans, drained and rinsed

1 × 400 g (14 oz) tin red kidney beans, drained and rinsed

2 × 400 g (14 oz) tins diced tomatoes

pinch of caster (superfine) sugar

toasted crusty bread, to serve

1. Heat the oil in a wide-based saucepan.

2. Add the onion and garlic and cook over a low heat for 10 minutes, adding a little water to stop them from browning.

3. Add the capsicum and paprika and cook for a further 5 minutes.

4. Add the remaining ingredients, together with 250 ml (8½ fl oz/1 cup) water. Bring to the boil, then reduce the heat and simmer for 40 minutes.

5. Adjust the seasoning and serve on toast. *If doubling up the recipe, split the mixture in two and allow the extra meal to cool to room temperature. Refrigerate overnight before freezing for later use.*

 VARIATION
Transfer the baked bean mix to an ovenproof dish and drop in eggs, then bake until the eggs are cooked. Sprinkle with feta and dried chilli flakes and serve. Allow 1 egg per person.

Falafel Fritters

Try this twist on traditional falafel. Pan-fried falafel fritters are a nice alternative to their deep-fried counterparts. The self-raising flour can be substituted with besan (chickpea) flour to make these fritters gluten-free.

Prep 30 minutes | Cook 30 minutes | Serves 4

2 × 400 g (14 oz) tins chickpeas, drained and rinsed, or 220 g (8 oz/1 cup) dried chickpeas, soaked and cooked (see Tip on page 138)

20 g (¾ oz/1 cup) flat-leaf (Italian) parsley, chopped

1 garlic clove, crushed

2 teaspoons ground cumin

1 teaspoon ground coriander

½ red onion, chopped

75 g (2¾ oz/½ cup) self-raising flour, plus extra flour for dusting

1 teaspoon salt

60 ml (2 fl oz/¼ cup) olive oil

4 Lebanese breads

400 g (14 oz/2 cups) Tabbouleh (page 201), or lettuce and tomato

100 g (3½ oz) plain or Greek yoghurt

tomato sauce (ketchup) or Sriracha sauce and hummus, to serve

1. Place one-quarter of the chickpeas in a food processor with the parsley, garlic, cumin, coriander and onion and blend to a paste.

2. Add the remaining chickpeas and pulse to add texture. They should be quite coarse.

3. Transfer the mixture to a bowl. Add the flour, then season with the salt and some pepper. The mix should be quite firm. *If doubling up the recipe, freeze one meal's worth of the mix at this point.*

4. Form the mixture into 10–12 patties and place on a baking tray sprinkled with flour.

5. Heat the oil in a non-stick frying pan over a medium–high heat and cook the patties until golden brown on both sides. If cooking in bulk, keep the cooked patties warm in the oven while you fry the rest.

6. Cut each of the breads in half and fill with falafel fritters, tabbouleh, yoghurt, tomato sauce and hummus.

 When cooking dried chickpeas, remove them when they are a little undercooked for a crisper finish to your fritters.

Fast & Fresh Meals

Meals that can be made from start to serving in one hour. Make two each week.

Asian Beef Mince

Wok cooking is a great way to prepare a meal in a short amount of time. This is a family favourite and can be on the table in minutes. Measure out all the sauces before you start cooking. You can always do the veg prep a day in advance.

Prep 20 minutes | Cook 15 minutes | Serves 4

1 quantity Perfect Steamed Rice (page 205), to serve

100 ml (3½ fl oz) shaoxing (Chinese rice wine)

2 tablespoons sweet soy sauce (kecap manis)

3 tablespoons light soy sauce

1 tablespoon brown sugar

pinch of ground cinnamon

1 tablespoon olive oil

4 spring onions (scallions), finely sliced, white and green parts separated

2 garlic cloves, crushed or grated

1 tablespoon grated fresh ginger

500 g (1 lb 2 oz) lean minced (ground) beef

½ red capsicum (bell pepper), cut into matchsticks

1 carrot, cut into matchsticks

300 g (10½ oz/4 cups) Chinese cabbage (wombok), shredded

pinch of dried chilli flakes

1. Steam the rice according to the recipe on page 205, or follow the packet instructions.

2. Mix together the shaoxing, sweet soy sauce, light soy sauce, sugar and cinnamon, and set aside.

3. Heat a large frying pan or wok, add the oil and cook the white part of the spring onions, the garlic and ginger until fragrant.

4. Add the beef mince and fry to brown, stirring continuously to break up any lumps. Cook until the liquid has evaporated, about 5 minutes.

5. Add the sauce mix, capsicum, carrot and cabbage to the pan and stir to combine.

6. Remove from the heat and top with the green spring onion and chilli flakes, if desired.

7. Serve immediately with rice.

The leaner the mince, the better the taste.

Use whatever cabbage you have at home.

Crumbed Chicken Thighs

Making your own crumbed chicken is so easy even the kids can cook it. We like to use chicken thighs as they are lovely and moist, however, you can also use chicken breast fillets. If using breast fillets, we recommend slicing them through horizontally to cook more evenly.

Prep 5 minutes | Cook 30 minutes | Serves 4

75 g (2¾ oz/½ cup) plain (all-purpose) flour

pinch of salt

2 eggs, beaten

200 g (7 oz/2 cups) dry breadcrumbs

600 g (1 lb 5 oz) boneless chicken thighs, fat trimmed

60 ml (2 fl oz/¼ cup) olive oil

vegetables or salad, to serve

lemon wedges, to serve

1. Preheat the oven to 180°C (350°F/Gas Mark 4).

2. Place a sheet of baking paper on a large baking tray.

3. Combine the flour and salt in one bowl. Place the eggs in a separate bowl next to the flour, and the breadcrumbs on a plate.

4. Dip each piece of chicken first in the flour, shaking off any excess, then in the egg wash, then crumb the thighs on both sides with the breadcrumbs and place on the lined baking tray.

5. Drizzle olive oil over the coated thighs on both sides, then place in the oven.

6. Bake for 10 minutes, then turn and bake for a further 10 minutes until golden and cooked through.

7. Serve with salad or vegetables and lemon wedges on the side.

 Make your own bread-crumbs from leftover stale bread and store in the freezer.

Stir-fried Mince with XO Sauce

XO sauce is a spicy sauce made from dried scallops, originating in Hong Kong. You can make this simple dish using any minced meat that you have available.

Prep 10 minutes | Cook 20 minutes | Serves 4

1 quantity Perfect Steamed Rice (page 205), to serve

1 tablespoon XO sauce

3 tablespoons light soy sauce

2 tablespoons shaoxing (Chinese rice wine)

1 tablespoon olive oil

500 g (1 lb 2 oz) minced (ground) pork or chicken

1 spring onion (scallion), finely sliced, white and green parts separated

1 carrot, grated

200 g (7 oz) semi-firm tofu, cubed

Steamed Asian Greens (page 205), to serve

1. Steam the rice according to the recipe on page 205, or follow packet instructions.

2. In a jug, combine the XO sauce, soy sauce, 3 tablespoons water and the shaoxing. Stir and set aside.

3. Heat the oil in a large frying pan or wok, add the meat and fry to brown, breaking it up as you go. Add the white part of the spring onion and the carrot. Continue to cook for a few minutes, then add the sauce from step 2.

4. Continue to cook and bring to the boil.

5. At this point, taste the meat and see if it needs another spoon of XO sauce. (Different brands have different levels of heat.)

6. Add the tofu and green parts of the spring onion and stir through.

7. Serve with rice and steamed greens.

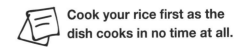

Cook your rice first as the dish cooks in no time at all.

Portuguese Butterflied Chicken

Portuguese chicken has a great flavour that everyone loves. You can easily make it at home with a few pantry staples and a whole chicken for a fraction of the cost of takeaway. We are cheating a little here, as you need to do the marinade in advance, when you get home from the shops. We also show you how to butterfly a chicken, but you can always ask the butcher to do this for you.

Prep 10 minutes | Cook 50 minutes + marinating time of 4+ hours | Serves 4–5

1 garlic clove, crushed or grated

1 tablespoon sweet paprika

1 tablespoon oregano leaves (fresh or dried)

¼ teaspoon dried chilli flakes

1 lemon, zested, then cut into wedges for serving

¼ teaspoon freshly cracked black pepper

60 ml (2 fl oz/¼ cup) olive oil

1.4 kg (3 lb 1 oz) whole chicken

salad or vegetables, to serve

1. Make the marinade by combining the garlic, paprika, oregano, chilli flakes, lemon zest, black pepper and olive oil. Place in a dish large enough to hold the butterflied chicken.

2. Butterfly the chicken (see opposite).

3. Rub the marinade under the skin of the breasts and all over the legs and bone side of the chicken.

4. Cover with plastic wrap and refrigerate for 4 hours, or overnight.

5. When ready to cook, heat a barbecue plate or large frying pan over a medium–high heat. Preheat the oven to 160°C (320°F/Gas Mark 3).

6. Remove the chicken from the fridge and sprinkle with salt on both sides.

7. Cook the chicken on the flat plate of the barbecue for 10 minutes, flesh side down. Flip and continue cooking for another 10 minutes.

8. Place the chicken in an ovenproof dish or tray and bake for an additional 20 minutes. Skewer the thickest part of the flesh to check that the juice runs clear. If not, continue to cook for a few more minutes.

9. Cover with foil and rest for 10 minutes. Cut into 6–8 pieces for serving.

10. Serve with salad or veggies and lemon wedges.

 If cooking for more than five people, cook two chickens rather than increasing the size of the chicken.

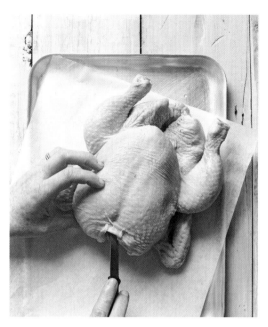
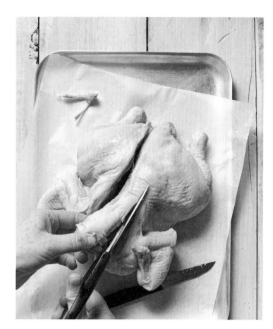
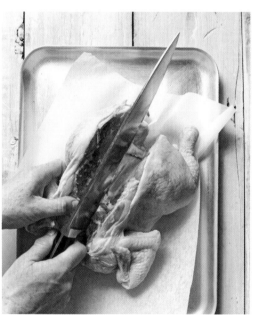

HOW TO BUTTERFLY A CHICKEN

1. Cut around the inside and outside of the wishbone and remove it with your hands.

2. Rest the chicken, breast-side down, on a chopping board or tray. Using kitchen scissors, cut along both sides of the spine and remove.

3. With the heal of the knife, split the breastplate near where you removed the wishbone. This will help flatten out the chicken and make it easier to cook on the barbecue.

4. Turn the chicken over and score the thighs and legs about three times on each side with a sharp knife.

Thai Pork Stir-fry

This is a super-quick meal. If you love curries but haven't got the time to slow-cook one, this Thai stir-fry is for you.

Prep 5 minutes | Cook 30 minutes | Serves 4

1 tablespoon olive oil

600 g (1 lb 5 oz) minced (ground) pork or chicken

2 teaspoons red curry paste

1 shallot, finely sliced

250 ml (8½ fl oz/1 cup) coconut cream

225 g (8 oz) tinned sliced bamboo shoots, drained and cut into matchsticks

1 tablespoon fish sauce

2 tablespoons brown sugar

4 kaffir lime leaves, 2 finely sliced, 2 left whole

1 quantity Perfect Steamed Rice (page 205), to serve

8 fresh coriander (cilantro) sprigs, leaves picked

1 cucumber, sliced

½ iceberg lettuce, finely sliced

1 lime or lemon, quartered

1. Heat the oil in a wok or large frying pan and sauté the meat until brown, breaking it up as you go.

2. Add the curry paste, shallot and coconut cream, and stir through.

3. Add the bamboo shoots, fish sauce, sugar and lime leaves. Bring to the boil, then reduce the heat and simmer for 20 minutes.

4. In the meantime, steam the rice according to the recipe on page 205, or follow the packet instructions.

5. After 20 minutes, check the meat mixture and adjust the seasoning with a little more fish sauce if required.

6. Serve with coriander, cucumber, lettuce, rice and lime or lemon wedges.

 Not all store-bought curry pastes are the same; some are saltier than others.

Eggplant Wraps

Looking longingly at those eggplants and wondering what to cook? Here is your answer. Crumbed eggplant is a staple in many countries. Here, we've made them into wraps that the whole family will enjoy.

Prep 10 minutes | Cook 30 minutes | Serves 4

1 eggplant (aubergine)

2 teaspoons of salt

60 g (2 oz) plain (all-purpose) flour

100 g (3½ oz/1 cup) dry breadcrumbs

2 eggs, lightly beaten

2 tablespoons olive oil

Lebanese bread

2 tomatoes, sliced

½ lettuce, shredded

tomato sauce (ketchup) or Sriracha, to serve

hummus, to serve (optional)

Yoghurt dip

250 g (9 oz/1 cup) plain or Greek yoghurt

1 zucchini (courgette), grated

½ garlic clove, crushed or grated

4 fresh mint sprigs, chopped

¼ teaspoon ground cumin

1. Slice the eggplant into 1 cm (½ in) rounds. Sprinkle with salt on both sides and place in a colander. Set aside for 10 minutes.

2. To make the yoghurt dip, combine all the ingredients in a bowl and refrigerate.

3. Rinse the salt off the eggplant and pat dry with paper towel.

4. Place the flour and breadcrumbs on separate plates. Place the eggs in a bowl.

5. Line up the plates in the order of flour, eggs, spare plate and then breadcrumbs.

6. Dip the eggplant first in the flour, shaking off any excess. Then pass it through the egg mix and then leave on the spare plate to drain.

7. Repeat with the remaining eggplant rounds, then crumb them in the breadcrumbs and set aside.

8. Heat a large frying pan over a medium heat. Add the olive oil and, once hot, place the crumbed eggplant in the pan (you may need to work in batches). Fry for 2–3 minutes until golden, then flip and cook for another 2 minutes on the other side.

9. Drain on paper towel. Serve warm, wrapped in Lebanese bread with tomato, lettuce, yoghurt dip, tomato sauce and hummus, if desired.

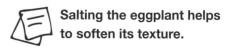

Salting the eggplant helps to soften its texture.

Pad Thai

Pad Thai is one of my favourite Thai dishes, but I often find it too oily. I am partial to a lot of chilli, so I serve the chilli on the side to dial up the heat for adults.

Prep 10 minutes | Cook 30 minutes | Serves 4

200 g (7 oz) rice stick noodles

2 tablespoons fish sauce

juice of 1 lime

1 tablespoon brown sugar

1 tablespoon tamarind purée

3 tablespoons olive oil

2 eggs, beaten

2 shallots, finely sliced

300 g (10½ oz) chicken breast, diced

1 teaspoon shrimp paste

1 carrot, finely grated

200 g (7 oz) firm tofu, diced

8 fresh coriander (cilantro) sprigs, leaves picked

1 tablespoon crispy fried shallots

1 tablespoon crushed peanuts, to serve

1 red finger chilli, finely sliced, to serve (optional)

1. Cook the noodles according to the packet instructions, then drain well.

2. Combine the fish sauce, lime juice, sugar and tamarind, then set aside.

3. Heat 1 tablespoon of the oil in a wok or a large, non-stick frying pan.

4. Add the egg and stir for 1–2 minutes until scrambled. Transfer to a bowl.

5. Wipe out the wok and, when the pan is really hot, add the remaining oil, followed by the shallot and chicken. Cook for 3 minutes, tossing continuously. Add the shrimp paste and cook until fragrant.

6. Add the carrot and tofu and cook for a further 2 minutes.

7. Add the noodles and sauce mixture from step 2.

8. When heated through, add the egg, coriander and crispy fried shallots.

9. Serve with peanuts and chilli on the side, if using.

Limes are in season in the cooler months, so it's a great idea to buy in bulk, juice them and freeze in ice cube trays for later use.

Fish with Salsa Verde

Salsa verde is a versatile accompaniment to salmon, white fish or other meats.

Prep 5 minutes | Cook 10 minutes | Serves 4

500 g (1 lb 2 oz) salmon or white fish fillets, cut into 4 pieces

steamed greens, to serve

lemon wedges, to serve

Salsa Verde

40 g (1½ oz/2 cups) flat-leaf (Italian) parsley, leaves picked

1 anchovy fillet

1 teaspoon capers

1 garlic clove

juice of ½ lemon

2 tablespoons olive oil

1. To make the salsa verde, combine all the ingredients in a food processor and blend for a few minutes.

2. Alternatively, make the salsa verde by hand. Chop the parsley until it is quite fine and place in a bowl. Add the finely chopped anchovies, capers and garlic along with the lemon juice and olive oil. Mix to combine and set aside until serving.

3. Pan-fry or barbecue the fish, turning once (the thicker the fish, the longer it takes – but generally less than 5 minutes a side).

4. Serve the fish with the salsa verde, steamed vegetables and lemon wedges on the side.

 The flavour will be sharp to taste but is balanced when drizzled on barbecued fish or meat.

Plan Buy Cook

Chicken Hokkien Noodles

This dish requires a bit of prep, but is super fast to cook. You can substitute the chicken with tofu if you prefer. A great all-in-one wok meal.

Prep 20 minutes | Cook 15 minutes | Serves 4

500 g (1 lb 2 oz) hokkien noodles

2 tablespoons sweet chilli sauce

3 tablespoons tomato sauce (ketchup)

2 tablespoons light soy sauce

1 tablespoon olive oil

1 red onion, sliced

1 garlic clove, finely grated

1 tablespoon sambal oelek

400 g (14 oz) chicken breast, diced

250 g (9 oz) green beans, halved

1 carrot, grated

1 red capsicum (bell pepper), finely
    sliced

1 tablespoon crispy fried shallots
    (available in Asian supermarkets)

1 lime, quartered

1. Place the noodles in a bowl and cover with boiling water. Leave for around 10 minutes (or follow the packet instructions), then strain.

2. Mix together sweet chilli sauce, tomato sauce, soy sauce and 2 tablespoons water in a bowl or jug and set aside.

3. Heat the oil in a wok or large frying pan and fry the onion and garlic for 2 minutes. Add the sambal oelek and chicken and cook, tossing constantly, over a high heat until the chicken is cooked through.

4. Add the green beans, carrot and capsicum and fry for another 2 minutes. Add an extra tablespoon water to aid the cooking process and stop the food from sticking.

5. Add the drained noodles to the wok, then pour in the sauce mixture. Toss together over a high heat until heated through.

6. Sprinkle with crispy fried shallots and serve immediately with lime wedges.

 Try diced firm tofu or egg as an alternative to the chicken. Buy the hokkien noodles in the refrigerated section of the supermarket.

Fettuccine Carbonara

There are some nights when you just need a meal on the table in 15 minutes. Fettuccine carbonara is one such meal. While many recipes finish this dish with cream, traditionally it is made without it. We add some rocket for a bit of extra zing. Dinner done.

Prep 5 minutes | Cook 10 minutes | Serves 4

2 eggs, beaten

100 g (3½ oz/1 cup) grated parmesan

4 flat-leaf (Italian) parsley sprigs, leaves picked, chopped

35 g (1¼ oz/1 cup) rocket (arugula)

1 tablespoon olive oil

2 garlic cloves, bruised

500 g (1 lb 2 oz) fettuccine

200 g (7 oz) bacon, diced

2 tablespoons white wine

1. Bring a large saucepan of salted water to the boil.

2. In a bowl, combine the egg, parmesan, some pepper, parsley and rocket and set aside.

3. Heat the oil in a large frying pan, add the bruised garlic and cook until fragrant and golden.

4. In the meantime, add the pasta to the boiling water and cook according to the packet instructions until al dente.

5. Remove the garlic from the oil, then add the bacon and fry until cooked to your liking (crispy or slightly softer). Once cooked, add the wine to the pan then remove from the heat.

6. Strain the pasta in a colander (keeping 60 ml (2 fl oz/¼ cup) of the cooking liquid aside in case it is needed for the sauce), then place the frying pan back over a medium heat.

7. Add the strained pasta to the pan and toss to combine with the bacon.

8. Add the egg mixture to the pan and immediately turn off the heat. Stir the egg mixture through the pasta and bacon, adding a splash of the cooking liquid if you need it to help stir through the egg. Serve immediately.

 Ask your deli to cut the bacon from the block (loin) as you can dice it yourself at home to your preferred thickness. You can also buy kaiserfleisch from the deli, which is also perfect.

Vegetable Stir-fry

Incorporating at least one vegetarian meal each week is a great way for families to keep introducing more vegetables to children's diets. Try not to eat all the cashews before the meal gets to the table.

Prep 15 minutes | Cook 20 minutes | Serves 4

1 quantity Perfect Steamed Rice (page 205), to serve

2 teaspoons white vinegar

80 ml (2½ fl oz/⅓ cup) oyster sauce

2 tablespoons shaoxing (Chinese rice wine)

2 teaspoons sesame oil

1 tablespoon olive oil

½ red onion, sliced

1 teaspoon grated fresh ginger

1 garlic clove, crushed or grated

2 carrots, sliced

1 red capsicum (bell pepper), sliced

280 g (10 oz/4 cups) broccoli, cut into small florets

120 g (4½ oz) green beans

1 tablespoon vegetable stock

120 g (4½ oz) sugar-snap peas, tips snipped

20 cashew nuts

1. Steam the rice according to the recipe on page 205, or follow the packet instructions.

2. Combine the vinegar, oyster sauce, shaoxing and sesame oil, then set aside.

3. Heat the olive oil in a wok or large frying pan over a high heat, and fry the onion, ginger and garlic until fragrant.

4. Add the carrot, capsicum, broccoli and green beans, and cook for 5 minutes.

5. Add the stock, then cover with a lid and cook for 5 minutes.

6. Remove the lid and add the sugar-snap peas and the sauce mix from step 2. Toss through.

7. Top the vegetables with cashew nuts and serve with the steamed rice.

 Use a vegan oyster sauce or omit to make this dish into a vegan meal.

Pastitsio

Pastitsio, also known as pasticcio, is a fabulously tasty macaroni lamb bake. It is like a Greek variation of macaroni cheese. It is worthwhile buying a whole nutmeg instead of using ground nutmeg, as it keeps its flavour better.

Prep 10 minutes | Cook 1 hour | Serves 4

1 tablespoon olive oil

1 onion, finely diced

500 g (1 lb 2 oz) minced (ground) lamb

½ teaspoon ground cinnamon

¼ teaspoon ground nutmeg or finely grated whole nutmeg, plus extra for sprinkling

½ teaspoon salt

100 g (3½ oz) tomato paste (concentrated purée)

250 g (9 oz) macaroni

green salad, to serve

White sauce

50 g (1¾ oz) butter

50 g (1¾ oz/⅓ cup) plain (all-purpose) flour

750 ml (25½ fl oz/3 cups) full-cream (whole) milk

¼ teaspoon salt

1. Heat the oil in a medium to large saucepan and cook the onion until soft.

2. Add the lamb and cook until brown, breaking up any lumps as you go.

3. Add the cinnamon, nutmeg, salt and tomato paste to the meat and cook for a few minutes, stirring continuously.

4. Add 250 ml (8½ fl oz/1 cup) water, bring to the boil, then reduce the heat and simmer for 30–40 minutes.

5. Cook the macaroni in a large saucepan of boiling salted water according to the packet instructions. Drain and set aside.

6. Preheat the oven to 180°C (350°F/Gas Mark 4).

7. To make the white sauce, melt the butter in a saucepan, then add the flour and cook out for a few minutes.

8. Gradually add the milk in small amounts, whisking continuously. Bring it back to the boil each time you add more milk.

9. Once thickened, add the salt and continue to cook over a low heat for 5 minutes (this helps cook out the flour). Set aside.

10. Place the macaroni in a 30 × 20 cm (12 × 8 in) baking dish.

11. Add the meat mixture and spread evenly over the top of the macaroni.

12. Pour the white sauce over the meat mixture, then sprinkle with extra nutmeg and cook in the oven for 20 minutes.

13. Serve immediately with a green salad.

 You can cook the meat the night before to save time. Reheat before assembling.

Plan Buy Cook

Fried Rice

Nothing beats fried rice for a great, speedy meal. Most of the ingredients are pantry and fridge staples, and you can even do a fair amount of the prep while the rice is steaming. Great for busy nights.

Prep 20 minutes | Cook 25 minutes | Serves 4

400 g (14 oz/2 cups) jasmine rice

2 tablespoons olive oil

2 eggs

½ onion, chopped

1 garlic clove, crushed or grated

1 teaspoon grated fresh ginger

4 rashers (slices) bacon, diced

2 tablespoons shaoxing (Chinese rice wine)

2 carrots, finely grated

200 g (7 oz/1 cup) corn kernels (tinned or frozen)

130 g (4½ oz/1 cup) frozen peas

80 ml (2½ fl oz/⅓ cup) oyster sauce

1. Place the rice in a saucepan, cover with 550 ml (18½ fl oz) water and bring to the boil. Cover and simmer for 12 minutes over a very low heat.

2. Remove the rice from the heat and allow to stand for 5 minutes without removing the lid as it continues to cook in its own heat.

3. Meanwhile, heat half the oil in a wok or large, non-stick frying pan. Break the eggs into the wok and scramble. Remove the eggs from the wok and set aside. Wipe out the wok with some paper towel.

4. Using the same wok, heat the other half of the oil and cook the onion, garlic, ginger and bacon until fragrant. Add a small amount of water to stop it sticking.

5. Add the shaoxing, carrot, corn, peas, egg and cooked rice. Stir continuously until heated through, about 1–2 minutes.

6. Finish by adding the oyster sauce. Stir to combine and serve.

 If reheating in the microwave, add a little water because the rice can get a bit dry when reheated.

San Choy Bau

San choy bau is a great meal for hot summer nights. Once washed, keep the lettuce leaves in the fridge for super-crisp freshness.

Prep 15 minutes | Cook 20 minutes | Serves 4

1 quantity Perfect Steamed Rice (page 205), to serve (optional)

1 tablespoon dried black fungus (optional)

1 iceberg lettuce

80 ml (2½ fl oz/⅓ cup) shaoxing (Chinese rice wine)

3 tablespoons light soy sauce

10 ml (¼ fl oz) sesame oil

1 tablespoon oyster sauce

1 teaspoon caster (superfine) sugar

1 tablespoon olive oil

2 teaspoons grated fresh ginger

2 spring onions (scallions), finely sliced

600 g (1 lb 5 oz) minced (ground) pork or chicken

80 g (2¾ oz/½ cup) water chestnuts, sliced

2 carrots, grated

8 fresh coriander (cilantro) sprigs, leaves picked

1. Steam the rice according to the recipe on page 205, if using, or follow packet instructions.

2. Place the black fungus, if using, in a heatproof bowl, cover with boiling water and leave to stand for 10 minutes. Drain and set aside.

3. Using a knife, remove the core from the iceberg lettuce. Carefully pull the lettuce apart into individual leaves and place in a bowl of water in the fridge. This helps the lettuce leaves to stay crisp and retain their shape.

4. Mix the shaoxing, soy sauce, sesame oil, oyster sauce and sugar in a bowl and set aside.

5. Heat the oil in a large frying pan or wok and cook the ginger and half the spring onions until fragrant.

6. Add the meat and cook until brown, about 5 minutes, breaking up any lumps as you go.

7. Add the water chestnuts and carrot, then stir through.

8. Add the sauce from step 4, combine thoroughly and remove from the heat.

9. Drain the lettuce leaves and pat dry with paper towel or a clean tea towel (dish towel).

10. Transfer the meat mixture to a serving dish, sprinkle with the coriander leaves and the remaining spring onion.

11. Spoon the meat into lettuce cups to serve, or serve with rice on the side for a more substantial meal.

 Make this meal vegetarian by substituting the meat with crumbled firm tofu.

Poached Chicken & Lamb with Rice

This is my version of a traditional Lebanese dish, and it's a surprisingly quick one to make. Add some grated garlic to the yoghurt for extra flavour when serving.

Prep 10 minutes | Cook 30 minutes | Serves 4

2 tablespoons slivered almonds

1 litre (34 fl oz/4 cups) chicken stock

1–2 × 150 g (5½ oz) chicken breasts

1 tablespoon olive oil

1 onion, finely diced

150 g (5½ oz) minced (ground) lamb

¼ teaspoon salt

½ teaspoon ground cinnamon

4 flat-leaf (Italian) parsley sprigs, leaves picked, chopped

400 g (14 oz/2 cups) jasmine rice

2 tablespoons currants

250 g (9 oz/1 cup) plain or Greek yoghurt

mixed salad leaves or steamed greens, to serve

1. Preheat the oven to 160°C (320°F/Gas Mark 3), scatter the almonds on a tray and lightly toast them for 5–10 minutes.

2. In a saucepan, bring the chicken stock to the boil, then add the chicken. Bring back to the boil, then reduce the heat and simmer for 15 minutes. Turn off the heat and leave the chicken in the pan until ready to serve.

3. Heat the oil in a wide-based saucepan and cook the onion for a few minutes. Add a little of the poaching liquid to moisten and prevent the onion from sticking.

4. Add the lamb and stir continuously to break up any lumps. When the lamb is browned, add the salt, cinnamon and parsley and cook for 3 minutes.

5. Add the rice to the lamb mixture and stir to combine.

6. Check the cooking instructions on the rice packet and add enough of the chicken poaching liquid to cook the rice (generally 200 g/7 oz/1 cup uncooked rice to 300 ml/10½ fl oz of liquid). If you need more liquid, use boiling water from the kettle.

7. Bring to the boil, cover with a lid and simmer over a very low heat for 12 minutes.

8. Turn off the heat (leaving the lid on) and allow the rice and lamb mixture to stand for 5–10 minutes.

9. To serve, mix the currants and almonds through the rice. Slice the chicken breast and place it on top. Serve with yoghurt on the side and salad or steamed greens.

 Use a simmer mat to ensure the even distribution of heat on gas cooktops for absorption cooking. While making this dish, poach extra chicken for lunches or the Vietnamese Chicken Salad on page 188.

Spanakopita

Spanakopita is a fantastic vegetarian dish the whole family can enjoy, and it's perfect for an occasion where you have lots of mouths to feed.

Prep 10 minutes | Cook 45 minutes | Serves 4

500 g (1 lb 2 oz) frozen spinach

1 tablespoon olive oil

1 onion, finely diced

1 garlic clove, crushed or grated

500 g (1 lb 2 oz/2 cups) firm ricotta

100 g (3½ oz) feta, crumbled

75 g (2¾ oz/¾ cup) grated parmesan

2 eggs

2 flat-leaf (Italian) parsley sprigs, leaves picked, chopped

½ teaspoon lemon zest

pinch of ground nutmeg

2–4 large sheets filo pastry

30 g (1 oz) butter, melted, or 1 extra tablespoon olive oil

1. Defrost the spinach then squeeze out any excess liquid.

2. Heat the oil in a saucepan and cook the onion and garlic until fragrant, about 10 minutes. Add a bit of water to stop the onion from colouring. Turn out onto a plate and allow to cool.

3. In a large bowl, mix together the ricotta, feta, parmesan, eggs, parsley, lemon zest, nutmeg and some pepper. Add the spinach and cooled onion mix to the bowl and stir to combine.

4. Preheat the oven to 180°C (350°F/Gas Mark 4).

5. Line the base of a 25 cm (10 in) round or 30 × 20 cm (12 × 8 in) rectangle ovenproof dish with two sheets of filo pastry. The edges should overhang the dish.

6. Spread the spinach and cheese filling evenly over the base, then fold in the overhanging edges of the pastry. Brush the edges with melted butter.

7. Place in the oven and bake for 30–40 minutes.

8. Remove from the oven and leave to stand for 15 minutes, then cut to serve. Cut the lemon used for the zest into wedges and serve on the side.

 You can use fresh English spinach if you prefer. Two bunches of spinach are equal to about 500 g (1 lb 2 oz) of frozen spinach. If using fresh spinach, wash, then place in a large frying pan and wilt. Drain in a colander, squeeze out any excess liquid and set aside. Chop when cooled.

Pesto

Homemade pesto takes minutes to make and is a great go-to meal with pasta for a busy night. Pesto is also tasty served on toast or in sandwiches. You can add a small amount of grated garlic for extra flavour. One clove is too much, as it can overpower the pesto.

Prep 5 minutes | Cook 10 minutes | Serves 4

60 g (2 oz/2 cups) basil, leaves picked

40 g (1½ oz) grated parmesan

2 tablespoons pine nuts

3 tablespoons olive oil

1 teaspoon lemon juice

pasta of your choice, to serve

1. Using either a food processor or hand-held blender, blend the basil, parmesan and pine nuts to a paste.

2. Gradually add the oil and lemon juice while continuing to blend. *If doubling the recipe, freeze half for later use. Remember to defrost it in the fridge and not the microwave.*

3. If serving with pasta, cook the pasta according to the packet instructions, then strain and mix with the pesto in a separate bowl. Use a tablespoon or two of the cooking water from the pasta to loosen the pesto if it is too thick.

 Store any leftover pine nuts in the freezer. If pine nuts are unavailable, soak a slice of bread in milk, squeeze out any excess milk, then blend in step 1.

Chicken Yakitori

Yakitori is Japanese-style chicken on a stick. The real plus for this dish is that you don't have to marinate the meat before you cook it, so it is a perfect Fast & Fresh meal for your weekly meal plan. The spring onions impart a subtle flavour. So, what are you waiting for?

Prep 5 minutes | Cook 40 minutes | Serves 4

12 bamboo skewers

100 ml (3½ fl oz) light soy sauce

100 ml (3½ fl oz) mirin

1 tablespoon caster (superfine) sugar

1 teaspoon sesame oil

1 quantity Perfect Steamed Rice (page 205), to serve (optional)

4 spring onions (scallions)

800 g (1 lb 12 oz) boneless chicken thighs

olive oil, for greasing

Steamed Asian Greens (page 205), to serve (optional)

salad of your choice, to serve

1. Soak the bamboo skewers in water for 20 minutes while preparing the meal.

2. Combine the soy sauce, mirin and sugar in a saucepan over a medium heat and reduce by half. This will take about 5–10 minutes. Take the saucepan off the heat and add the sesame oil.

3. If using, steam the rice according to the recipe on page 205, or follow the packet instructions.

4. Cut the white part of the spring onions into 2 cm (¾ in) pieces (the soft green bits tend to burn, so keep them for use in another dish).

5. Cut the chicken into bite-sized pieces and thread onto the skewers, starting with a piece of chicken, then spring onion, and so forth, finishing with chicken. Brush the skewers with a little marinade.

6. Heat a barbecue plate or large frying pan over a low heat. Grease the barbecue plate with some oil and cook the chicken slowly, turning and basting as you go, for about 10–15 minutes. Close the lid of the barbecue between each turn.

7. Remove the skewers from the barbecue and place in a dish, then use a clean brush to brush with the remaining marinade on both sides. Cover with foil and leave to rest for 5 minutes.

8. Serve with steamed Asian greens, or salad and rice.

 This is a great way to use up leftover spring onions that you can never seem to find a use for before they go limp.

Haloumi & Pumpkin Fritters

These moreish fritters make a great sandwich filling and are also delicious tossed through a salad with rocket, beetroot, mint and yoghurt. However you eat them, they are so tasty you'll want to make them often.

**Prep 10 minutes | Cook 30 minutes |
Makes 16 fritters**

250 g (9 oz) haloumi cheese, grated

300 g (10½ oz) butternut pumpkin (squash), grated

2 spring onions (scallions), finely sliced

1 egg

75 g (2¾ oz/½ cup) self-raising flour

½ teaspoon ground cumin

¼ teaspoon salt

2 tablespoons olive oil

250 g (9 oz/1 cup) plain or Greek yoghurt

4 fresh mint sprigs, leaves picked, chopped

bread or rolls, to serve

rocket (arugula) or salad leaves, to serve

fresh cooked baby beetroot (beets), sliced, to serve

1. Mix the grated haloumi, pumpkin, spring onions, egg, flour, cumin and salt in a bowl until combined.

2. Heat the oil in a frying pan and place spoonfuls of the mixture into the pan. Cook over a medium heat until golden, then turn and cook until golden on the other side. Keep the fritters warm in a low oven while you cook the rest.

3. Combine the yoghurt and chopped mint in a bowl.

4. To serve, toast the bread then top with rocket, fritters, sliced beetroot and mint yoghurt.

 If you can't find fresh cooked beetroot in the vegetable section of your supermarket, use tinned beetroot instead.

Fried Vermicelli Noodles

This fried vermicelli noodle recipe is a great way to use up leftover vegetables from the fridge at the end of the week. Ready in minutes, it is perfect for a night when you have very little time. Look out: it will become your go-to quick dinner very soon.

Prep 10 minutes | Cook 10 minutes | Serves 4

¼ teaspoon ground turmeric

2 tablespoons light soy sauce

2 tablespoons sweet soy sauce (kecap manis)

240 g (8½ oz) dried vermicelli rice noodles

2 tablespoons olive oil

2 eggs, lightly beaten

1 teaspoon sambal oelek or red curry paste

2 spring onions (scallions), white and green parts separated, finely sliced

1 teaspoon grated fresh ginger

bunch of broccolini, cut into batons (or any leftover veg from the fridge)

2 carrots, grated

1 red or green capsicum (bell pepper), sliced

2 tablespoons peanuts, chopped (optional)

1. Mix together the turmeric, soy sauce, sweet soy sauce and 2 tablespoons water. Set aside.

2. Cook the noodles according to the packet instructions, then strain in a colander and refresh under cold water.

3. Heat half the oil in a large frying pan or wok. Add the eggs, then move them continuously with a spatula until scrambled. Remove from the pan and set aside.

4. Clean the wok and heat the remaining oil. Add the sambal oelek, the white part of the spring onions and the ginger, and cook until fragrant.

5. Add the broccolini, carrot, capsicum, noodles and sauce mix from step 1. Stir continuously until well combined, then add the cooked egg.

6. Sprinkle with the green part of the spring onions and peanuts (if using). Serve immediately.

You can use any dried noodles you have in the pantry for this dish.

Udon Noodles

This Japanese-inspired noodle dish is another fast meal. If you don't have pickled ginger, the dish is still great without it, but it does round it off nicely.

Prep 15 minutes | Cook 15 minutes | Serves 4

4 carrots, grated

1 green capsicum (bell pepper), sliced

4 field mushrooms, sliced

2 eggs

80 ml (2½ fl oz/⅓ cup) light soy sauce

1 tablespoon mirin

1 teaspoon sesame oil

1 tablespoon olive oil

400 g (14 oz) udon noodles

2 spring onions (scallions), finely sliced

1 tablespoon pickled ginger, finely sliced

1 teaspoon toasted sesame seeds

Dressing

80 ml (2½ fl oz/⅓ cup) mirin

2 tablespoons rice vinegar

dash of sesame oil

2 tablespoons light soy sauce

1. Combine all the ingredients for the dressing in a small bowl and set aside.

2. Combine the carrot, capsicum and mushrooms in a large bowl.

3. Add the eggs, soy sauce, mirin and sesame oil, and mix well.

4. Heat the olive oil in a wok or large frying pan over medium–high heat.

5. Add the vegetable mix and stir continuously for 2–3 minutes until the egg starts to set.

6. Add the noodles and keep stirring until they are heated through.

7. Remove from the heat and add the dressing from step 1.

8. Serve sprinkled with spring onions, pickled ginger and toasted sesame seeds.

 Udon noodles can be found pre-cooked in the Asian section of the supermarket.

Fish Cakes

I prefer these fish cakes to the store-bought, deep-fried ones. Not only do they taste better, but they look better too. Basa fillets, which are widely available in supermarkets, work well with this recipe.

Prep 15 minutes | Cook 30 minutes | Serves 4

1 quantity Perfect Steamed Rice (page 205), to serve

600 g (1 lb 5 oz) white fish fillets, skin removed

1 tablespoon red curry paste

100 g (3½ oz) green beans, finely sliced

4 kaffir lime leaves, finely sliced

1 teaspoon caster (superfine) sugar

2 tablespoons fish sauce

2 tablespoons olive oil

Steamed Asian Greens (page 205) or salad, to serve

red finger chilli, sliced, to garnish (optional)

Dipping sauce

1 teaspoon light soy sauce

3 tablespoons white vinegar

2 tablespoons caster (superfine) sugar

1 shallot, finely sliced

½ Lebanese (short) cucumber, diced

2 cm (¾ in) piece fresh ginger, peeled and cut into matchsticks

4 fresh coriander (cilantro) sprigs, leaves picked (optional)

1. Preheat the oven to 160°C (320°F/Gas Mark 3).

2. Steam the rice according to the recipe on page 205, or follow the packet instructions.

3. For the fish cakes, blend the fish and curry paste to a smooth paste in a food processor (dice the fish first if required). Be careful not to overprocess the mix as it gets too aerated. Transfer to a bowl.

4. Add the beans, kaffir lime leaf, sugar and fish sauce.

5. Mix thoroughly, then form into patties (having wet hands helps to make the patties smooth).

6. To make the dipping sauce, combine the soy sauce, vinegar and sugar and 2 tablespoons water in a small saucepan. Heat over a low heat until the sugar dissolves. Remove from the heat and set aside to cool.

7. Place the shallot, cucumber, ginger and coriander leaves, if using, in a bowl.

8. When the dipping sauce has cooled, add it to the cucumber mix. Stir and set aside.

9. Heat a non-stick frying pan with the oil. Lightly brown the fish cakes on each side, transfer to a baking tray and cook in the oven for 5–8 minutes.

10. Serve with dipping sauce, veggies or salad and rice. Garnish with sliced chilli, if desired.

If you are time poor, forget the dipping sauce and serve with steamed rice, veggies and a store-bought sweet chilli sauce instead.

Tex-mex Rice & Corn

My kids love Mexican food. I'm always looking for dishes the whole family will enjoy, and this tasty vegetarian dish does not disappoint. I serve it with plain or Greek yoghurt, but of course the kids prefer sour cream.

Prep 5 minutes | Cook 40 minutes | Serves 4

2 corn cobs

2 tablespoons olive oil

1 onion, finely diced

1 teaspoon cumin seeds

2 tablespoons tomato paste (concentrated purée)

400 g (14 oz/2 cups) jasmine rice

500 ml (17 fl oz/2 cups) chicken or vegetable stock

2 × 400 g (14 oz) tins black beans, drained and rinsed

2 chipotle peppers in adobo sauce (see Note)

8 fresh coriander (cilantro) sprigs, leaves picked

plain or Greek yoghurt, or sour cream, to serve

1. Bring a large saucepan of water to the boil, then add the corn cobs. Boil until tender, about 30 minutes if cooking from fresh. Once the corn is cooked, set aside.

2. While the corn is cooking, heat the oil in a heavy, wide-based saucepan. Cook the onion without colouring it. Add the cumin seeds and cook for a couple of minutes until fragrant, then add the tomato paste. Cook for 2 minutes, stirring continually.

3. Add the rice and combine well.

4. Pour in the stock, then add the beans and the chipotle peppers.

5. Bring to the boil, then place a piece of baking paper on the surface of the mixture, cover with a lid and simmer for 12–15 minutes.

6. Turn off the heat and allow the rice to sit for 5 minutes before removing the lid.

7. Stir the rice and remove the two chipotle peppers.

8. Serve with fresh coriander, yoghurt or sour cream and the corn cobs.

 Chipotle peppers in adobo sauce are available at most supermarkets in the Mexican section. Freeze any remaining chipotle and sauce for next time.

Thai Beef Salad

Thai basil, with its slightly aniseed flavour, is one of my favourite Asian herbs. If you can't find it, use Vietnamese mint instead.

Prep 20 minutes | Cook 20 minutes | Serves 4

2 tablespoons fish sauce

500 g (1 lb 2 oz) beef rump

200 g (7 oz) green beans, halved

bunch of broccolini, halved

½ red capsicum (bell pepper), cut into matchsticks

8 Thai basil sprigs, leaves picked

8 fresh coriander (cilantro) sprigs, leaves picked

1 shallot, finely sliced

1 tablespoon crispy fried shallots

olive oil, for greasing

pinch of dried chilli flakes

lime wedges, to serve

Dressing

3 tablespoons fish sauce

3 tablespoons rice vinegar

2 tablespoons caster (superfine) sugar

1 garlic clove, crushed or grated

juice of 1 lime

1. Pour the fish sauce over the beef and allow it to marinate for at least 15 minutes.

2. Blanch the green beans and broccolini by cooking them in boiling water for 2 minutes. Drain and refresh in cold water.

3. Combine the beans, broccolini, capsicum, Thai basil, coriander, shallot and crispy fried shallots in a large bowl.

4. Combine all the dressing ingredients with 125 ml (4 fl oz/½ cup) water and set aside.

5. Heat a barbecue chargrill plate or chargrill pan over a very high heat. Rub the plate or bars with a little oil on some paper towel.

6. Barbecue the beef until cooked to your preference.

7. Transfer to a warm plate, cover with foil and rest for 10 minutes.

8. Slice the beef finely, then add to the salad ingredients, pour over the dressing and top with dried chilli flakes. Serve with lime wedges on the side.

You can add extra vegetables, such as shredded cabbage, to this salad. Serve with steamed rice (page 205) for a more substantial meal.

Vietnamese Chicken Salad

The dressing for this salad is my go-to over summer. Don't be put off by the fish sauce; it makes a tasty base for the dressing and is well balanced by the other flavours. You can use fresh chilli instead of dried chilli flakes if you have it.

Prep 15 minutes | Cook 30 minutes | Serves 4

400 g (14 oz) chicken breast

1 garlic clove, peeled

2 tablespoons fish sauce

450 g (1 lb/6 cups) Chinese cabbage (wombok), shredded

2 carrots, finely sliced

2 shallots, finely sliced

4 fresh mint sprigs, leaves picked

4 fresh coriander (cilantro) sprigs, leaves picked

½ red capsicum (bell pepper), finely sliced

pinch of dried chilli flakes

1 tablespoon crispy fried shallots

Dressing

3 tablespoons fish sauce

3 tablespoons rice vinegar

2 tablespoons caster (superfine) sugar

juice of 1 lime

1 garlic clove, crushed or grated

1. To make the dressing, combine all the ingredients with 125 ml (4 fl oz/½ cup) water and set aside.

2. In a small saucepan, place the chicken breast, garlic, fish sauce and enough water to cover the chicken.

3. Bring to the boil, then reduce the heat and simmer for 15 minutes. Once cooked, leave the chicken in the liquid.

4. Combine the cabbage, carrot, shallot, mint, coriander and capsicum in a bowl.

5. Remove the chicken from the poaching liquid and shred using a fork. Add it to the salad, then pour over the dressing.

6. Serve with dried chilli flakes and crispy fried shallot.

You could use a store-bought barbecue chicken for a fast salad. Serve with steamed rice (page 205) for a larger meal.

Niçoise Salad

A great summer dinner or lunch. The oil from the tuna with lemon juice makes the dressing, simplifying the process.

Prep 5 minutes | Cook 25 minutes | Serves 4

8 chat potatoes

4 eggs

200 g (7 oz) green beans

2 baby cos (romaine) lettuces, rinsed and chopped

425 g (15 oz) tuna in oil

4 roma tomatoes, quartered

12 kalamata olives, pitted

juice of 1 lemon

1. Place the potatoes in a small saucepan of cold water and bring to the boil. Reduce the heat and simmer until tender, about 15 minutes. Strain, then slice or quarter.

2. Meanwhile, in a separate small saucepan, boil some water, then gently lower the eggs into it. Simmer for 8–9 minutes.

3. Strain the eggs, immediately immerse them in cold water, then peel before they cool. Cut the eggs lengthways into wedges.

4. Blanch the green beans in boiling salted water for 2–3 minutes, then drain and immediately refresh in ice-cold water. Set aside.

5. To assemble, place the potatoes, green beans, lettuce, tuna with its oil, tomatoes, olives, lemon juice and some salt and pepper in a bowl and lightly toss.

6. Divide between four plates or bowls, then top with the eggs.

Add 1 tablespoon mayonnaise with the lemon juice in step 5 if you prefer.

Soba Noodle Salad

Soba is the Japanese name for buckwheat. This is one of those lovely summer salads that are perfect for a hot evening. It still tastes great the next day, even when dressed. You may just need to add a handful of extra spinach leaves or greens to bulk it out.

Prep 25 minutes | Cook 15 minutes | Serves 4

4 spring onions (scallions), finely sliced

2 carrots, grated

½ red capsicum (bell pepper), finely sliced

100 g (3½ oz) snow peas (mangetout), blanched and sliced

100 g (3½ oz/2 cups) baby spinach

4 fresh mint sprigs, leaves picked

4 fresh coriander (cilantro) sprigs, leaves picked

180 g (6½ oz) dried soba noodles

1 tablespoon crispy fried shallots

1 teaspoon toasted sesame seeds (see Note)

Dressing

100 ml (3½ fl oz) light soy sauce

2 tablespoons sesame oil

2 teaspoons caster (superfine) sugar

1 garlic clove, crushed or grated

1 tablespoon grated fresh ginger

1. To make the dressing, combine all ingredients in a small bowl with 200 ml (7 fl oz) water. Set aside.

2. Combine the spring onion, carrot, capsicum, snow peas, spinach, mint and coriander in a large bowl.

3. Bring a large saucepan of water to the boil and cook the soba noodles according to the packet instructions, then drain and rinse under cold water.

4. Add the noodles to the bowl.

5. Pour over the dressing and mix through.

6. Sprinkle with crispy fried shallots and toasted sesame seeds.

 Not all soba noodles are gluten-free. Check the packet if serving to anyone with a gluten intolerance.

Toast your sesame seeds in a hot, dry frying pan. Move them around continuously until golden.

Linda's Chicken Gumbo

(GF)

Linda is my friend Erika from America's mum. She makes this dish with okra, which is often hard to come by. I've exchanged the okra for green beans, but if you find okra, fresh or frozen, give it a try.

Prep 20 minutes | Cook 45 minutes | Serves 4

2 corn cobs, husks removed

2 tablespoons olive oil

1 onion, finely diced

1 celery stalk, finely diced

600 g (1 lb 5 oz) boneless chicken thighs

1 × 400 g (14 oz) tin diced tomatoes

500 ml (17 fl oz/2 cups) chicken stock

50 g (1¾ oz/¼ cup) jasmine rice

200 g (7 oz) green beans, halved

2 pinches of dried chilli flakes

1. Place the corn cobs in a saucepan of salted water and bring to the boil. Reduce the heat and simmer corn for 30 minutes.

2. Meanwhile, heat the oil in a large saucepan. Add the onion and celery and cook for 5 minutes, then add the chicken and brown on all sides.

3. Add the tomatoes, chicken stock, a pinch of salt and some pepper. Ensure the chicken is just covered with liquid. If not, top it up with some water. Bring to the boil and simmer, uncovered, for 20 minutes.

4. Meanwhile, slice the corn off the cob and add it to the chicken.

5. Add the rice and cook for a further 15 minutes, adding the green beans in the last 5 minutes of cooking time.

6. Adjust the seasoning and serve with dried chilli flakes on the side.

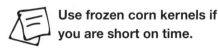 **Use frozen corn kernels if you are short on time.**

BBQ Salads

Pick two salads and whip up a leafy green salad to accompany barbecued meats for a gathering.

Greek Salad

Our Greek salad uses dried Greek oregano, which is available at specialty delis or supermarkets. If you can't find it in the shops, simply leave it out. I like to keep feta in brine as a fridge staple, as it keeps for a long time.

Prep 10 minutes | Cook 5 minutes | Serves 4

½ shallot, finely sliced

½ red capsicum (bell pepper), diced

½ yellow capsicum (bell pepper), diced

1 Lebanese (short) cucumber, diced

250 g (9 oz) cherry tomatoes, halved

12 kalamata olives, pitted

2 flat-leaf (Italian) parsley sprigs, leaves picked

2 basil sprigs, leaves picked

¼ teaspoon dried Greek oregano

100 g (3½ oz) feta, crumbled

1 tablespoon red-wine vinegar

1 tablespoon olive oil

1. Combine all the ingredients with some pepper in a large bowl and mix well.

2. Place on a serving platter and serve at room temperature.

See image on page 197.

 The different capsicums add nice colour to this dish, but it's equally fine to just use one whole red capsicum if you have it.

Italian Potato Salad

Italian potato salad uses red-wine vinegar and olive oil as a dressing. Serve at room temperature. For a vegetarian version, omit the anchovies and add more capers.

Prep 10 minutes | Cook 30 minutes | Serves 4

600 g (1 lb 5 oz) chat potatoes

½ shallot, finely diced

2 teaspoons capers, rinsed

2 anchovy fillets, smashed

6 flat-leaf (Italian) parsley sprigs, leaves picked, chopped

2 teaspoons red-wine vinegar

1 tablespoon extra-virgin olive oil

1. Place the potatoes in a saucepan and cover with salted cold water. Bring to the boil, then reduce the heat and simmer, uncovered, for 25 minutes, or until tender.

2. Combine the remaining ingredients in a large bowl with some seasoning to make the dressing.

3. Once the potatoes are cooked, cut each into quarters (or halves for smaller ones), then add them to the dressing mix and toss to combine. The potatoes should be hot to absorb all the dressing.

4. Check for seasoning and add more salt and pepper if required. Serve at room temperature.

   See image on page 197.

Beetroot Salad

You can buy peeled and cooked beetroot in the refrigerator section of the supermarket, or use tinned baby beetroot if you can't find fresh.

Prep 5 minutes | Cook 5 minutes | Serves 4

80 g (2¾ oz/4 cups) rocket (arugula)

4 cooked baby beetroots (beets), quartered

100 g (3½ oz) feta

4 fresh mint sprigs, leaves picked

1 tablespoon balsamic vinegar

2 tablespoons extra-virgin olive oil

1. Combine the rocket, beetroot, feta and mint in a bowl.

2. Add the balsamic vinegar and olive oil with a sprinkle of sea salt.

3. Toss gently and place on a serving platter.

   See image on page 196.

 A great salad to accompany lamb, or served with other salads as a light meal.

Plan Buy Cook

Asian Coleslaw

The freshness of the mint and green apple sets this apart from other coleslaw recipes. It's great with any marinated or barbecued meats.

Prep 15 minutes | Cook 1 minute | Serves 4

150 g (5½ oz/2 cups) savoy cabbage, shredded

150 g (5½ oz/2 cups) purple cabbage, shredded

2 carrots, grated

8 fresh mint sprigs, leaves torn or chopped

1 shallot, finely sliced

1 green apple, grated

juice of 1 lime or lemon

½ teaspoon sesame oil

¼ teaspoon salt

1. Combine the cabbages, carrot, mint, shallot and green apple in a bowl and toss together.

2. Add the lime juice, sesame oil and salt, toss to combine, then serve.

   See image on page 196.

 Use a hand-held slicer or mandoline to shred the cabbage quickly.

Caprese Salad

Traditionally made with sliced buffalo mozzarella, our modern take on this Italian classic uses bocconcini for an easy alternative.

Prep 5 minutes | Cook 5 minutes | Serves 4

400 g (14 oz) mixed, colourful tomatoes

250 g (9 oz) cherry tomatoes

200 g (7 oz) bocconcini

8 fresh basil sprigs

balsamic vinegar and extra-virgin olive oil, for drizzling

1. Cut the larger tomatoes into quarters and the cherry tomatoes in half, then place in a bowl.

2. Tear the bocconcini balls into bite-sized pieces and add them to the bowl.

3. Add the basil, toss gently and place on a platter or serving plate.

4. Drizzle with balsamic vinegar, olive oil, salt and pepper and serve.

   See image on page 197.

Quinoa Salad

I love to serve this salad with the Portuguese Butterflied Chicken (page 152) and a leafy salad. It could also be made with brown rice if you don't have quinoa.

Prep 15 minutes | Cook 30 minutes | Serves 8

4 corn cobs, husks removed

400 g (14 oz/2 cups) quinoa

1 celery stalk, diced

1 red capsicum (bell pepper), diced

1 Lebanese (short) cucumber, diced

100 g (3½ oz/2 cups) baby spinach

2 shallots, finely diced

bunch of fresh coriander (cilantro), leaves picked

juice of 2 limes

pinch of dried chilli flakes (optional)

1. Place the corn in a saucepan of salted water and bring to the boil. Reduce the heat and simmer for 30 minutes.

2. Drain the corn and allow to cool, then slice off the kernels and discard the cobs.

3. Meanwhile, place the quinoa in a saucepan with plenty of salted water. Bring to the boil, then reduce the heat and simmer, uncovered, for 10–15 minutes, or until the grains are tender. The 'tail' of the quinoa pops out when it is cooked. Drain and leave to cool.

4. Combine the celery, capsicum, cucumber, spinach, shallot, coriander, corn and quinoa in a serving bowl.

5. Add the lime juice and season with salt and pepper.

6. Serve with dried chilli flakes, if desired.

 We use (and prefer) white quinoa in this dish.

Tabbouleh

Cutting the parsley by hand gives a lovely texture to this tabbouleh recipe. Team this up with our Lamb Kibbeh (page 97) or Falafel Fritters (page 143) for a great meal.

Prep 10 minutes | Cook 20 minutes | Serves 4

90 g (3 oz/½ cup) burghul (bulgur wheat)

40 g (1½ oz/2 cups) flat-leaf (Italian) parsley, leaves picked

1 tomato, diced

1 shallot, finely diced

juice of 1 lemon

¼ teaspoon salt

1. Place the burghul in a bowl. Cover with cold water and soak for 20 minutes.

2. Rinse and drain the burghul, squeezing out any excess water using the back of a spoon.

3. While the burghul is soaking, chop the parsley finely.

4. Combine the burghul with the rest of the ingredients and adjust the seasoning to taste.

5. Serve with kibbeh or falafel, or as a salad with barbecued meats.

 Use brown rice or freekeh as a substitute for burghul if unavailable.

Pumpkin & Couscous Salad

This is great as a summer salad when entertaining, and goes well with Mango Chicken (page 126). You can cook the pumpkin in advance and simply reheat it in the oven before tossing with the remaining ingredients when you are serving the salad.

Prep 20 minutes | Cook 45 minutes | Serves 6–8

2 tablespoons slivered almonds

500 g (1 lb 2 oz) pumpkin, diced

1 onion, diced

2 teaspoons ground coriander

2 teaspoons ground cumin

¼ teaspoon salt

olive oil, for drizzling

200 g (7 oz/1 cup) couscous

125 ml (4 fl oz/½ cup) boiling water

1 × 400 g (14 oz) tin chickpeas, drained and rinsed

200 g (7 oz) cherry tomatoes, halved

½ bunch of fresh coriander (cilantro), leaves picked

5 flat-leaf (Italian) parsley sprigs, leaves picked, chopped

250 g (9 oz/1 cup) plain or Greek yoghurt, to serve

1. Preheat the oven to 180°C (350°F/Gas Mark 4).

2. Spread the almonds on a baking tray lined with baking paper. Place in the oven and cook for 5–10 minutes, or until golden.

3. Mix the pumpkin, onion, coriander, cumin, salt and olive oil together in a bowl, then spread out on a baking tray lined with baking paper.

4. Roast for 25 minutes, or until the pumpkin is soft.

5. Place the couscous in a heatproof bowl and cover with the boiling water. Stir continuously with a fork, breaking up any lumps.

6. Cover the bowl with plastic wrap and cook in the microwave for 1–2 minutes on a medium heat. If you don't have a microwave, see our couscous recipe on page 206 for a stovetop method.

7. Combine the couscous, chickpeas, tomatoes, coriander, parsley and roasted pumpkin. Transfer to a serving plate and sprinkle with the toasted almonds.

8. Serve with the yoghurt.

This is the perfect salad when entertaining a large crowd.

You can cook the almonds and pumpkin at the same time, just remember to remove the nuts from the oven ahead of the pumpkin.

Speedy Sides

Perfect Steamed Rice

Want a failproof method to steam rice to perfection? Here it is in five easy steps.

Prep 2 minutes | Cook 20 minutes | Serves 4–6

400 g (14 oz/2 cups) long grain rice (we like jasmine, generally, but basmati is also good)

1. Rinse the rice in a colander.
2. Put the rice in a medium saucepan and cover with 550 ml (18 fl oz/2¼ cups). Bring to a rapid boil.
3. Once boiling, cover the saucepan with a tight-fitting lid and turn down the heat to very low. Cook for 12 minutes.
4. After 12 minutes, turn off the heat, leaving the lid on the saucepan. Leave to stand for 5 minutes.
5. Remove the lid, fluff the rice with a fork and serve.

 If you cook the rice a little early, just leave it to stand with the lid on until you're ready to serve. This way, it will retain its heat better.

If your pot lid doesn't fit tightly, use some foil under the lid to trap the steam while cooking.

Steamed Asian Greens

You can't go past a quick steamed veg side. Cook this in a saucepan or a wok for a ready-in-minutes side for any Asian-inspired meal.

Prep 2 minutes | Cook 5 minutes | Serves 4

4 baby bok choy (pak choy), quartered (you can also use choy sum or gai lan)

Dressing (optional)

1 teaspoon sesame oil

1 tablespoon light soy sauce

1 teaspoon toasted sesame seeds

1. Bring a large saucepan of salted water to the boil.
2. Wash the quartered bok choy to remove any grit, then place in the saucepan.
3. Return to the boil, then strain after 2 minutes.
4. Serve the bok choy as is, or make the dressing by combining all ingredients in a bowl with 1 tablespoon water before drizzling over the bok choy.

DID YOU KNOW?

When boiling root vegetables such as potato, sweet potato and carrot, start the vegetables in cold water.

For non-root vegetables such as corn, beans and broccoli, cook the veg in boiling water.

Failsafe Couscous

Couscous is a great addition to salads, as a side to tagines or with our barbecued lamb (page 129). This recipe ensures you have light and fluffy couscous every time.

Prep 2 minutes | Cook 5 minutes | Serves 4

370 g (13 oz/2 cups) couscous
180 ml (6½ fl oz/¾ cup) boiling water

Microwave

1. Place the couscous in a microwave-safe bowl with a pinch of salt and pepper.

2. Pour the boiling water (from the kettle) over the couscous. Continuously stir the grains with a fork until all the water is absorbed and the grains have separated. At this point, if the couscous appears dry, you may need to add a little extra boiling water.

3. Cover and microwave on a medium–high heat for 1 minute.

4. Remove from the microwave, then mix with a fork to break up any clumps.

Stovetop

1. Half-fill a saucepan with water and bring to the boil.

2. Meanwhile, combine the 180 ml (6½ fl oz/¾ cup) boiling water with the couscous in a bowl. Continuously stir the grains with a fork until all the water is absorbed and the grains have separated.

3. Tip the couscous into a sieve and place the sieve on top of the saucepan on the stove. Cover the sieve with a lid. The water should not touch the bottom of the sieve.

4. Steam for 5–10 minutes until light and fluffy, then serve.

Don't Forget the Veggies

We all need more veg in our diet, so plan for at least two veggies on the side each night. Offer them in the middle of the table or before dinner as snacks for the kids while preparing the main meal.

Prep time: 5 minutes | Cook 30 minutes | Serves 4

2 corn cobs, husks removed

4 carrots, cut into sticks

300 g (10½ oz) green beans, tails removed

1 broccoli head, cut into florets, stem peeled and sliced

1. Bring a saucepan of water to the boil, then add the corn cobs. Reduce the heat, cover with a lid and cook the cobs for about 30 minutes.

2. To cook the carrot, place it in a saucepan with cold water. Add a pinch of salt and bring to the boil, then simmer for 15 minutes.

3. To cook the beans or broccoli, bring a saucepan of water to the boil. Add a pinch of salt, then add the beans or broccoli. Bring back to the boil, then cook to your liking, about 5 minutes.

Cabbage Salad

This simple salad is great with pork dishes, Crumbed Chicken Thighs (page 148) or Portuguese Butterflied Chicken (page 152).

Prep 10 minutes | Cook 1 minute | Serves 4–6

300 g (10½ oz/4 cups) savoy cabbage, shredded

4 red radishes, finely sliced

1 shallot, finely sliced

20 g (¾ oz/1 cup) flat-leaf (Italian) parsley, leaves picked

juice of 1 lemon

1 tablespoon mayonnaise

Combine all the ingredients and serve immediately.

Our Go-to Salad Dressing

Serves 4

Make a dressing by combining 2 tablespoons white Italian condiment (also known as white balsamic vinegar), 2 tablespoons olive oil and a generous pinch of salt, then toss over a mixed leafy green salad. Adjust the vinegar for personal preference.

Super
Simple
Meals

Super simple meals are life savers. Make one each week. So simple, anyone can make them.

Flatbread Pizzas

Store Lebanese bread in the freezer to make these pizzas as a quick snack or a Super Simple meal.

Preheat your oven to 200°C (400°F/Gas Mark 5). Top the bread with some tomato passata (puréed tomatoes) and cheese for the fastest option, or use any leftover Napolitana Sauce (page 114), then add your own ingredients to use up any leftover veggies e.g. capsicum (bell peppers), mushrooms or leftover roasted vegetables, and top with cheese. Mozzarella works well, grated or sliced.

Sausages & Mash

So simple it doesn't need much explanation.

Buy some sausages, potatoes and green veg. Fry the sausages while boiling the peeled potatoes. Cook the green veg as you like. Mash the potatoes with some milk and butter or olive oil. Easy.

BLTs or BLATs

Bacon, lettuce and tomato sandwiches – what's not to like? For a BLAT, add some avocado.

Fry the bacon, slice the rolls or toast the bread, then serve with lettuce, tomato and avocado if you are feeling fancy, plus some mayonnaise. Spice it up with Sriracha if you like it hot.

Jacket Potatoes

Microwave, bake or boil the potatoes, then fill them with your favourite ingredients. Put them under the grill to melt the cheese, if using. If you want to bake the potatoes from scratch, remember to allow at least 1 hour for cooking (which kind of eliminates the super simple or fast bit). We like to use boiled chat potatoes, as they take so much less time to cook.

Use any ingredients you like:

- baked beans and cheese
- tuna, peas and corn
- bacon, avocado and cheese
- corn, spinach and bacon

Top with sour cream or plain or Greek yoghurt.

Toasted Sandwiches

Whether you use a sandwich press or a frying pan to toast your sandwiches, a little butter on the outside of the bread gives it a lovely, golden brown colour.

Great fillings include:

- ham and cheese (and tomato)
- pesto, tomato and cheese
- tinned sardines
- avocado and feta

We like to add the tomato after the sandwiches have been toasted, to avoid those mouth-burning incidents, and to keep it fresh.

Steak Sandwiches

Pretty much as per BLTs, except with a piece of steak. You can always add some caramelised onion if you have it on hand or in the freezer. Add cheese, of course, and any other ingredients that you like, such as sliced beetroot.

HOW TO CARAMELISE ONIONS

Slice about 4–8 onions, add ½ teaspoon of salt, then cook in a heavy-based saucepan over a low heat with some olive oil for about 30–40 minutes, or until golden. Stir regularly. The onion should caramelise on the base of the pan. Stirring will give an even, golden colour. Store in the freezer until ready to use. If you make them in bulk, you'll have plenty on hand for Super Simple meal nights.

Eggs, Four Ways

Learning to cook eggs is a valuable skill to keep you powered up with protein. Poached, fried, scrambled or boiled: they are a great start or end to the day. Here, we show you how to cook perfect eggs four ways.

POACHED

Bring a saucepan or frying pan of water to the boil, then add 1 teaspoon vinegar. Break the eggs into individual ramekins, being careful not to pierce the yolks. Stir the water to create a whirlpool. Drop the eggs into the just boiling water, one at a time, then, just before the water comes back to boil, reduce the heat to medium. Once the eggs float to the top, they are ready. Remove with a slotted spoon and drain on paper towel before serving on toast.

BOILED

You may like a soft-boiled egg, or perhaps you like your eggs hard-boiled. It all comes down to the cooking time. Bring a saucepan of water to the boil. Carefully place the eggs, one at a time, into the saucepan using a spoon. Cook them for 4–5 minutes for runny eggs, about 7 minutes for soft-boiled eggs, and 9 minutes for hard-boiled eggs. Times will vary depending on the size of your eggs, and whether the eggs are from the fridge or at room temperature.

SCRAMBLED

For a quick scramble, melt 1 tablespoon butter in a non-stick frying pan over a high heat. Whisk two eggs and 3 tablespoons milk together. Pour the egg mixture into the hot pan once the butter is bubbling nicely. Leave for about 20 seconds, then stir with a silicone spatula. Leave for a further 20 seconds, then stir again. Cook the eggs for another 20 seconds, or until they are cooked to your liking. Season with salt and pepper and serve immediately with sourdough toast and other accompaniments.

FRIED

To fry eggs, heat a frying pan over a high heat and add 1 tablespoon oil or butter. Break the eggs into the frying pan, reduce the heat, then sprinkle with a bit of salt. Cook to your liking, spooning over some of the oil to cook the top of the egg.

SIDES
Eggs any way are great served with toast (soldiers for boiled eggs), smashed avocado or wilted spinach, sautéed mushrooms and bacon.

Omelette

Nothing beats a meal as easy as this omelette. Once you have perfected the technique, there are loads of filling options to suit all tastes.

Prep 5 minutes | Cook 2 minutes | Serves 1

2 eggs

1 tablespoon olive oil or 20 g (¾ oz) butter

fresh herbs, such as chives or flat-leaf (Italian) parsley, finely chopped (optional)

Filling options:

- ham, cheese and tomato
- smoked trout and wilted rocket (arugula)
- cheese, tomato and baby spinach
- mushrooms fried in butter with feta

1. Prepare any filling ingredients (e.g. grated cheese, diced ham and tomato).

2. Crack the eggs into a bowl and whisk with a fork. Season with salt.

3. Heat a frying pan over a medium heat. Add the olive oil or butter once hot.

4. Pour in the eggs and, using a heatproof spatula, move them around the pan quickly.

5. When the eggs are set on the bottom and still a little runny on top, place the filling on half of the omelette, opposite the handle.

6. Fold the other side two-thirds of the way over the top of the filling.

7. Gently 'shuffle' the omelette to the front of the pan, then carefully roll the omelette out of the pan onto a plate to fully close it.

8. Serve with crusty toast and some fresh herbs, if using.

Asian Omelette

Try this Asian omelette variation to use your leftover vegetables.

Prep 10 minutes | Cook 10 minutes | Serves 1

1 teaspoon olive oil

½ carrot, grated

1 × 10 cm (4 in) piece of celery, cut into matchsticks

2–4 snow peas (mangetout), cut into matchsticks

pinch of grated fresh ginger

pinch of grated garlic

1 teaspoon oyster sauce

20 g (¾ oz/¼ cup) bean sprouts

drop of sesame oil

2 eggs, beaten

lime wedges, to serve (optional)

1. Heat the oil in a small frying or omelette pan, and cook the carrot, celery, snow peas, ginger and garlic for 3–4 minutes. Add a drop of water if it begins to stick.

2. Add the oyster sauce, bean sprouts and sesame oil to the vegetable mixture and stir through.

3. Tip the vegetable mix into a bowl and set aside.

4. Wash out the same frying pan, then cook the omelette as per the Omelette recipe (page 214), adding the vegetable mix for the filling.

5. If making more than one omelette, cook all the vegetables together, but still cook the omelettes one at a time.

 Don't be put off if you don't have all these veggies; use whatever you have in the bottom of the veggie drawer at the end of the week.

About the PlanBuyCook App

PlanBuyCook is a real-life meal planner: use any of our 130 recipes or write your own favourites. You can also schedule in events such as eating out, leftovers, Foodbanked meals or takeaway – just like you plan your meals in real life.

SCALE YOUR MEALS

The PlanBuyCook app automatically scales recipes to match your household size, from 1 to 10 serves. You can easily double up freezable meal recipes to match your 4+2+1 plan.

ADD YOUR OWN RECIPES

Write your own recipes and the ingredients will automatically be added to the shopping list and aggregated along with any PlanBuyCook recipe ingredients you choose. The PlanBuyCook app will automatically scale your recipes to your household size or lock the scaling for desserts or recipes you do not wish to scale.

GENERATES A SHOPPING LIST LIKE MAGIC

The PlanBuyCook smart shopping list includes all meal ingredients, plus you can add everyday items that are automatically sorted by grocery section. Mark off items you already have in your fridge or pantry or edit amounts of each ingredient. Cross off the items as you shop. You can also send the shopping list to someone else.

The app comes with more than 130 everyday PlanBuyCook dinner recipes, plus freezable lunchbox snack recipes, all using ingredients available in the supermarket.

- Plan up to three meals a day
- Choose either metric or imperial measurements and the names of ingredients
- Features a real-life planner integrated with your calendar that can be shared between household members
- Smart shopping list, including 1200 everyday shopping items for both food and household
- Built-in timers
- Support from planbuycook.com.au

At planbuycook.com.au, we provide helpful planning and cooking tips along with kitchen basics (such as how-to videos) to help you find economical ways to feed your household and save time in the kitchen.

No more 'What's for dinner?'
Plan your meals, shop once – dinner done.
Go to www.appstore.com/planbuycook

Index

Thank You

We'd like to thank all our PlanBuyCook app users and workshop attendees, who have given us incredibly valuable feedback about our app and recipes since the launch. We love hearing how meal planning has worked for you and which recipes are on high rotation at your house. We have learnt so much from you along the way.

To our Hardie Grant team, publisher Jane Willson and MD Roxy Ryan for really backing our book, and Anna Collett for making it happen. And to Andrea O'Connor for your meticulous text editing, Bec Hudson and Georgia Young for your lovely photography and styling seen throughout, and Vaughan Mossop for the great book design.

Our friends and families have been with us all the way on this journey. From the initial idea through to now, we thank you for sticking with us and believing in us, and for all the ideas you have brought to the table along with feedback on our recipes (and the loan of dishes for photo shoots). It is no mean feat to bring an app and a book to the market, and we thank you deeply.

To Eddie, Lachlan and Lucy, and Simon, Luca, Alex and Evan – we'd never have been here without you. Both of us have fussy eaters in our houses (we won't name names), so to please them has been a challenge and a learning experience. We have funded this business without any external investment, so the support when it was all outgoing and little incoming was vital.

> Number of times Gaby procrastibaked during the writing of this book:
> 3 times a week (or more)

> Words that Jen banned from this book:
> Casserole
> Forage
> Soil
> Smear
> Deconstructed

To Simon, who has also been our tech adviser, app fixer-upper and general go-to person, words cannot express our gratitude. Your patience with us has been limitless, and you have worked tirelessly on the app at night time while working full-time elsewhere. One day, you might even get paid.

To our initial app crew: photographer Samara Clifford, designer Louise Brinkmann and developer Scott Ashton – you have all had an impact on our product's look, feel and functionality, which has remained fresh several years down the track.

Candice Meisels, you are a publicity machine and have been instrumental in our business success – thank you.

Our app, and now book, had very humble beginnings as a simple idea of two people who wanted to help others. It is a thrill to think that we now have a successful app and a book to help ease the load, bring tasty home cooking into people's lives and reduce their food waste.

We hope this book helps you and we encourage you to give us feedback and ideas at info@planbuycook.com.au. We will reply, and it will come directly from us and not a virtual assistant (mainly because we don't have one – yet).

Now stop reading and get dinner done – it will change your life.

Jen and Gaby

Published in 2020 by Hardie Grant Books,
an imprint of Hardie Grant Publishing

Hardie Grant Books (Melbourne)
Building 1, 658 Church Street
Richmond, Victoria 3121

Hardie Grant Books (London)
5th & 6th Floors
52–54 Southwark Street
London SE1 1UN

hardiegrantbooks.com

All rights reserved. No part of this publication may be reproduced,
stored in a retrieval system or transmitted in any form by any means,
electronic, mechanical, photocopying, recording or otherwise, without
the prior written permission of the publishers and copyright holders.

The moral rights of the authors have been asserted.

Copyright text © Jen Petrovic and Gaby Chapman 2020
Copyright photography © Bec Hudson 2020, except page 35
© Gaby Chapman 2020
Copyright illustrations © Vaughan Mossop 2020, except cover, page 14
(top and bottom), page 54 © Louise Brinkman 2020, page 14 (middle)
© Anton Banulski 2020
Copyright design © Hardie Grant Publishing 2020

 A catalogue record for this
book is available from the
National Library of Australia

The Plan Buy Cook Book
ISBN 978 1 74379 564 4

Publishing Director: Jane Willson
Project Editor: Anna Collett
Editor: Andrea O'Connor @ Asterisk & Octopus
Designer: Vaughan Mossop
Photographer: Bec Hudson
Illustrator: Vaughan Mossop, Louise Brinkman, Anton Banulski
Stylist: Georgia Young
Production Manager: Todd Rechner
Production Coordinator: Mietta Yans

Colour reproduction by Splitting Image Colour Studio
Printed in China by Leo Paper Products LTD.